PRAISE FOR *SLAY THE DRAGON*

"A well needed tool in a role that's regularly overlooked or thought of as an afterthought. In games, the player may be king, but if that's true, then story is a prince. And this book will make sure your prince will make it to the castle to slay the dragon!"
—**TIM LANG**, lead designer, *Might and Magic IX*, owner, Brrapp Games

"A comprehensive but accessible guide for those striving to relate to the medium of video games from another entertainment medium. If you're a writer from film or TV and want to understand more about games, this book should get you comfortable quickly."
—**DAN BOUTROS**, executive producer, *The Walking Dead Assault*; co-founder, Soul Arcade

"A great read for any storyteller, whether you're new to writing or just new to video games."
—**GRETCHEN MCNEIL**, author of *Ten* and the *Don't Get Mad* novels

"*Slay the Dragon* is brimming with real-world experience. It distills the lessons learned from the long, messy process of game development into concentrated form, guiding the reader to the intellectual tools needed to craft successful interactive narrative."
—**DAROLD HIGA, PHD**, producer, Wargaming.net

"*Slay the Dragon* is a very clear, concise, and h~~~~~ t every developer—or game writer—shoulc
—**JAY OBERNOLTE**, president, FarSight

D1248853

"If you ever wanted to know wha: were afraid to ask, this book is for you. I ~~~~~ received a clear answer, this book is for you too. If you are considering pursuing a writing career in games, this book is *definitely* for you."
—**DORIAN RICHARD**, lead writer & narrative designer

"The authors have created a wonderful map to help find your way out of your vault, through the wastelands, and into paradise. *Slay the Dragon* is the Konami Code for writers!"
—**KEITH TRALINS**, founder of MegaGigaOmniCorp, Inc., producer and game designer of *Lost, Twilight, The Walking Dead*, and *Take It All*

"Bridges the gap between traditional narrative and non-linear storytelling and makes it simple. A required tool in the working writer's toolbox."

—**PHILIP EISNER,** screenwriter, *Event Horizon*; consulting writer for Telltale Games, *Tales from the Borderlands*

"Game writers are everywhere. *Slay the Dragon* helps those who pursue it at any place around the world, be it in the US, Sweden, or anywhere else. It speaks to a global audience, and deserves to be read by everyone who is serious about game writing."

—**MARTIN HAGVALL,** lecturer in Media Arts, Aesthetics and Narration, University of Skövde (Sweden Game Arena)

"Having worked in both the realms of linear and interactive entertainment, the authors provide screenwriters with the techniques and insight they need to effectively cross over to a brave new world where players must become their writing companions."

—**DAVID MULLICH,** development director, *Heroes of Might & Magic III*; *I Have No Mouth, and I Must Scream*.

"An essential read for anyone interested in writing for video games or expanding their view of the entertainment industry. Gaming novices and experts alike will benefit from adding this book to their library."

—**SUE JOHNSON,** producer, Emmy-award winning Web series, *What If...*; scriptwriter, video game consultant

"What *Slay the Dragon* does best is get to the point. Readers be warned— once you have taken the Red Pill of truth for crafting tales, you will not look at media the same way again."

—**SCOTT NICHOLSON,** professor of game design, Wilfrid Laurier University; designer of *Going, Going, Gone* and *Tulipmania 1637*

"I've voiced-acted in over 200 games, and I've never found a book that details the importance of great characters to good dialogue as much as *Slay the Dragon*."

—**KAREN STRASSMAN,** actor, HBO's *Silicon Valley*, *Mortal Kombat X*, *StarCraft II: Heart of the Swarm*

"Immerses its readers in the world of video game writing. Comprehensive, up-to-the-minute, and loaded with great "beta tested" exercises that really work, this book is a must-have for aspiring game writers and fans alike!"

—**LINDA VENIS, PHD,** director, Department of the Arts and The Writers' Program at UCLA Extension

SLAY THE DRAGON

WRITING

GREAT VIDEO GAMES

Robert Denton Bryant & Keith Giglio

MICHAEL WIESE PRODUCTIONS

Published by Michael Wiese Productions
12400 Ventura Blvd. #1111
Studio City, CA 91604
(818) 379-8799, (818) 986-3408 (Fax)
mw@mwp.com
www.mwp.com
Manufactured in the United States
of America

Library of Congress Cataloging-in-Publication Data

Bryant, Robert Denton, 1963-
 Slay the dragon : writing great video games / by Robert
Denton Bryant & Keith Giglio.
    pages cm
 ISBN 978-1-61593-229-0
1. Video games—Authorship. I. Giglio, Keith, 1963-
II. Title.
 GV1469.34.A97B79 2015
 794.8—dc23
                              2015010503

Cover design by Johnny Ink. johnnyink.com
Interior design by Debbie Berne
Copyediting by David Wright

CONTENTS

Our Grateful Acknowledgements

Firstly, we want to thank you for buying this book. For putting your quarter in the arcade machine. We hope we inspire you to write, produce, or work on a great video game that elevates the industry to an even higher standard.

As this book is co-written, Keith and Bob have some co-thank you's. As a team, thank you to Ken Lee and Michael Wiese for believing in this book and opening up the video game world to their wonderful audience and network of amazing writers. Thank you David Wright for your mad copyediting skillz and for helping us to upgrade this book to epic quality. Thank you Debbie Berne for making our musings and doodles look awesome. Thank you to Linda Venis and Chae Ko at the UCLA Extension Writers' Program for giving us a classroom and allowing us to fill it with like-minded dreamers. Thank you to our research assistant, Stephen Warren, and to Alice Art Design and Rae Yamamoto for help with the graphics. And a special thank you to Larry "Major Nelson" Hryb for penning the Foreword.

I, Keith, would like to thank the other pieces on my game board of life: Juliet, Sabrina, and Ava. We've come a long way from that crazy night of playing *Risk!* Games often have a winner, and I am the winner with all of you in my life. Thanks to everyone at Syracuse University for supporting me in and out of the classroom. Especially to my chairman, Michael Schoonmaker, for getting our class on the books and to Dean Lorraine Branham for not telling me I'm crazy with some of my crazy ideas. Lastly, I want to thank Robert Sternberg. My friend. It's always a treat to have you around the house and firing up the Xbox. But more than that—thank you for letting me pick your brain about what you are playing; what you think is working in games and why. I hope your passion turns into your profession.

And I, Bob, would like to thank my Golden Globe-winning girlfriend Terri DePaolo for putting up with a lot—*a lot*—during the writing and researching of this book. Also to my former colleagues and lifelong friends Karen McMullan, Martin Hagvall, St.John Colón, Amy Zimmitti, Mike Dawson, Allen Im, Jennifer Estaris, Daniel Boutros, Jeffrey Kessler, Greg Morchower, David Mullich, Bill Smith, and Michael Blackledge for making me feel welcome and for teaching me to teach. Plus huge thanks to all of my students and "knuckleheads," past and present, for teaching me more than I ever taught you. I dedicate my effort in this book to my goddaughter Kristen Ericksen, who was playing *Gran Turismo* using manual transmission at age three, and who remains my favorite gamer.

Foreword

by Larry Hryb, Xbox Live's "Major Nelson"

VIDEO GAMES are big business. As you will soon learn (if you don't know already) the video game industry is HUGE. When I tell people that the industry I work in is a BILLION dollar business—they are amazed. I then follow up with another factoid: It's bigger than Hollywood. That's right. At only 44 years old, sales of the video game industry regularly eclipse the 125-year-old motion picture industry.

Yeah. That big.

While I've always been "into" video games—from that first time I played *Pong* at the local Sears department store on their "Video Arcade" system (just a re-branded version of the venerable Atari 2600) to the countless hours spent after school at friends' houses playing *NFL Football* on Intellivision—which was really nothing more than a series of dots on a screen. We had to IMAGINE that they were QBs, linebackers, etc. Hours and hours pushing dots around the screen with our hands and our imaginations.

I attended the Newhouse School of Communications at Syracuse University to study television, radio, and film production. There, I learned about traditional story development and using technology to bring ideas and characters to life: Write a script, go to the studio and shoot it with very expensive (tube) cameras, VTRs, etc. I practiced the art of storytelling, character arc, and all the hallmarks that make for a good linear story and program. I would study that by day, and return to my dorm in the evening and play video games. (It was upstate New York. What else was a nerd to do in the winter?) I could FEEL the creative and technical fields were on a crash course in gaming.

One day we would have video games with the fidelity of movies and TV. One day there would be far away worlds we could explore for hours on end.

Fortunately, we did not have to wait too long.

I started working on the Xbox team in late 2003—when we were deep into planning "Xenon," the console that would become the Xbox 360. I was working on the "platform" (the systems that games run on) with some of the smartest people I have ever worked with: software developers, testers, network engineers, hardware engineers, and more. ALL incredibly smart and talented, but VASTLY different from the creative environment I studied in and was used to. These men and women WERE the left brain. I was used to the warm, fuzzy, vague, right-brain way of thinking—but that was *not* what this was. I learned to measure, analyze, and make data-driven decisions, not just ones that "felt right."

I also got my first look into game development.

The next building over from where I worked was a studio named Bungie that Microsoft had purchased a few years earlier. They were working on *Halo 2*, a follow-up to their massively successful game *Halo* for the original Xbox. I would often go over there for meetings and I noticed something: The lines between technical and creative were just not there. It was one team of about one hundred people in a huge U-shaped room who were all creative *and* technical, sitting next to each other and coming up with creative ideas and making them "real" with computer code. Right before my eyes I saw something amazing: The two disciplines were working closely together to create that magical world I dreamt of years before while at Syracuse.

But, it was slightly different. As this book will show you, television, films, and radio are linear storytelling. The viewer (or listener) passively sits back and watches (or listens) to the story play out at a prescribed pace and with deliberately chosen camera angles and movements. In video games, it's completely different. The players are at the center of the action. THEY decide when and where to move, look, and take action. They can spend ten minutes in a hallway. Or ten seconds. The players can open this door, then that door, then go out this window. Or they can just go out another window. Maybe they turn around and go around the building. The pace and direction are entirely up to the players. This non-linear interactive storytelling is one of the many innovations that video games have created.

The book you are holding in your hands is for anyone who wants to learn about this new way of storytelling that really is an evolution of traditional storytelling. If you've written a screenplay—this book is for you. If you've ever played a video game and thought, "Hey, I have a great idea for a story"—this book is for you. If you want to get a better understanding of the multi-billion-dollar industry that is now a massive cultural and economic force—this book is for you.

I love video games. I love that a person playing a game can create stories and character connections with deep emotions that can be greater than movies. When I played *Red Dead Redemption*—an incredibly popular open-world game set in the great American West in the late 1800s—at the end I cried.

My wife walked into the room when I finished the game and she asked, "What's wrong?" All I could muster up was the ability to point at the screen and say "It's over. It's finally over."

We've all felt a little something at the ending of a good book or a movie, but this felt deeper. It was MY character I was controlling. I was the one that made the story go forward at my pace. I got to know the main character, John Marston, so well because I was controlling him. In many ways, I became John Marston. Especially after the countless hours of gameplay and story decisions I had made. When I got to the end it was overwhelming. (I won't spoil it for you but if you finished the game, you probably had the same experience.)

In linear storytelling, the story and character arcs are straightforward and the ending is the same for everyone, and in video games that can often be the case. But it becomes much more personal, since in video games you actually control the character and pace of the story.

Video games often allow the player to control the *direction* of the narrative, and in some games the outcome is directly based on in-game choices you, the player, have made. Video games can employ some extremely sophisticated storytelling where three different people playing the same game can have three different experiences and results based on their own in-game decisions. Very powerful stuff.

This book will show you what a game is and explore story and game genre, plot, character development, and much, much more. In my years of working in the industry this is the closest thing to a bible of creative video game story creation as I have ever seen. This is an amazing industry that I am proud to be a part of where you really can make your own real life adventure. Anything can happen. I love telling my old Syracuse classmates that I came to Microsoft and I was part of a team that won not one, but THREE Emmy Awards. A real life Emmy Award for working in the video game industry. That's how far we've come. (Kudos to the National Academy of Television Arts & Sciences for recognizing the importance and power of video game technology.)

Enjoy this book. Enjoy the journey of creating your stories and characters and making them come to life in a game for players around the world to (hopefully) enjoy.

I hope we get to meet someday and you can tell me about your own wonder and successes in the industry.

All the best,
Larry Hryb
Twitter: @majornelson
Seattle, Washington
February 2015

LOADING . . .

When Desmond Miles is kidnapped by a sinister corporation, they use a machine to send his consciousness back in time, where he is forced to re-live the adventures of his ancestors—a secret society of assassins. Can Desmond survive and stop the evil company's plans to change history?

After his airplane crashes in the middle of the Atlantic, Jack discovers a man-made underwater Utopia called "Rapture." But the city has gone mad: its gene-splicing-addicted citizens attack him, monstrous "Big Daddies" try to kill him on sight, and Rapture's autocratic founder will stop at nothing to maintain control. Can Jack escape to the surface before he becomes an unwitting pawn in this sub-marine madhouse?

After landing on a gargantuan, ring-shaped planet, the Master Chief, a genetically enhanced super-soldier, must battle a fanatical civilization known as the Covenant. Can he stop them before they can use their super weapon to destroy all life in the galaxy?

DO THESE BLURBS sound like the plots of Hollywood's upcoming summer blockbusters? They easily could be. Each of these story lines forms the basis of a multi-million-dollar franchise with a global audience, shelves full of licensed merchandise, legions of cosplaying fans, and side-stories in multiple media.

But these are NOT the plots of movies coming to a theater near you (not at the time of this writing, anyway, although *Halo: Nightfall* is a TV series). These are the story lines, worlds, and characters of blockbuster video games: *Assassin's Creed, BioShock,* and *Halo.* They are huge franchises born from video game stories. These games are interactive narratives that take place in very rich worlds populated with involving characters that inspire players to continue to interact and explore even after they've "beat the game." Video game stories and characters—their intellectual property (or "IP")—are the next great frontier of our collective pop culture imagination. Video games have finally come of age. Great stories are being told.

We've only mentioned three so far, but you can probably name many more: *Call of Duty, Borderlands, Resident Evil, Metal Gear Solid, Grand Theft Auto, Final Fantasy,* and *God of War.*

Does that list seem too hardcore?

Let's not forget the billions of dollars amassed by such family-friendly game franchises as *Skylanders, Angry Birds, Plants vs. Zombies, Professor Layton, Ratchet & Clank,* and *Clash of Clans.* That list goes on and on as well.

Where did this all start? When did games become more than games and a place where great stories might be told? Just as the movies can be traced back to the success of a lovable tramp, we think the first "box-office star" . . . the Charlie Chaplin of the arcades . . . was a plumber who helped to launch a thousand quarters, quests, multiple sub-franchises and a billion dollar industry: MARIO!

WOOT! A.K.A. WOW, LOOT!

Consumers in North America spent over $21 billion on games at retail last year,[1] and that's just on traditional "games-in-a-box" played with game consoles and personal computers. Worldwide and across all platforms, including mobile and tablet games, the number has been estimated at

---

1 Entertainment Software Association, *Essential Facts about the Computer and Video Game Industry 2014*, p. 13. http://www.theesa.com/facts/pdfs/ESA_EF_2014.pdf

$93 billion.[2] (We're not great with big numbers, but here's a comparison: for the same period, worldwide theatrical box office revenue was $35.9 billion.[3]) Even though thousands of "free to play" games are available nowadays, passionate players are still willing to spend big on games that engage them.

Furthermore, *everyone plays video games now.* Think about that. Video games have been around for almost 50(!) years, and for much of that time games have been made for and played by teenage boys. But we play games at all ages now: Roughly a third of gamers are younger than 18, a little more than a third are older than 36, and the remaining third are in the 18–35 year range. And the gender breakdown is almost even: 48% female, 52% male.[4]

The audience for games has exploded in the last 10 years, with the advent of touch-screen smartphones and tablets, as well as easy-to-use download stores like Apple's App Store, Google Play, and Steam. And we can't forget Nintendo's million-unit-selling Wii console, whose ground-breaking wiggle stick controllers helped thousands of parents and grandparents to play video games—many for the first time. But while more people than ever are playing video games, not everyone identifies themselves as a "gamer." (And that's okay. We'll discuss this later on.)

With this huge and diverse audience playing games, some Cassandras are now foretelling the END OF HOLLYWOOD AS WE KNOW IT.

It is not. Video games (and interactive fiction) are merely the latest media for writers to use their storytelling skills. We have a generation that has grown up with games. The Xbox has replaced the cable box. Hollywood is not going anywhere, but neither are video games. We believe that—just as television learned from film and film learned from television—it is time to examine the similarities and differences between games and film as storytelling media. The new writers in Hollywood have grown up with games in their homes and in their

---

2 http://www.gartner.com/newsroom/id/2614915

3 http://boxofficemojo.com/news/?id=3805&p=.htm

4 Entertainment Software Association, p. 3.

purses. From mobile to desktop, games are part of the pop culture conversation.

The emerging and the established writer in Hollywood—or who dreams of Hollywood, or dreams of storytelling anywhere in the world— should know how interactive narrative adds to the conversation and adds to the content.

A CRIMINALLY BRIEF HISTORY OF STORYTELLING TECHNOLOGY

Writers have always been drawn to new tech. From cave walls to the printing press—if there is a new way of delivering a story, storytellers will (usually) embrace it. Gutenberg's press was first used to print the Bible, but many other works soon followed. As books grew less expensive over time, newspapers, magazines, and "dime novels" were even cheaper—as they were designed to be mass-produced and distributed as widely as possible. Charles Dickens—a master of serialized storytelling and therefore the great-grandfather of binge watching—delivered his novels one chapter at a time in cheap, disposable weekly or monthly magazines. Devoted fans of his work and his characters would bark at him as he walked through London: *What have you in store for poor Pip?*

When radio emerged as a mass medium, writers began scripting radio plays: comedies, mysteries, science-fiction, adventure, melodramas . . . you name it. Families gathered around the radio each night and listened to stories (and sometimes musical numbers). Orson Welles, who had made his name as a stage director, used this new medium in a legendary way when he staged H. G. Wells's *The War of the Worlds* as a radio play, without telling the audience it was a play. America thought they were listening to a music program when the performance was interrupted with a special news report: Martians were invading the Earth via Grover's Mill, New Jersey. Welles's cleverly disguised narrative made use of then-familiar radio tropes to cause a national panic, if only for one night.

Remember those two names: Welles and Wells.

When film arrived around the turn of the twentieth century, it was a novelty. Early projections of trains coming into a station alarmed viewers. Wanderers in penny arcades would put coins into kinetoscopes to watch what we would now think of as animated .GIFs. (*BioShock Infinite* uses a silent movie within the game to tell part of the story. The machine the player sees it on: a kinetoscope.)

But there were no *stories* on film . . . until very short fiction films began to appear, like Edwin S. Porter's twelve-minute *The Great Train Robbery* (1903). Audiences (groups of people watching together, rather than the lonely experience of the kinetoscope) sat on benches or chairs in tents, or in theaters. Barely a dozen years later D. W. Griffith's incredibly successful (and incredibly racist) *The Birth of a Nation* (1915) proved that longer, "feature-length" movies were a viable means of telling longer, more complex, and multi-threaded stories. Even silent movies needed writers (or "scenarists"). Someone had to conceive the plot and write the intertitles.

Movies came of age in 1939. This was the beginning of Hollywood's golden age. Why 1939? The years 1939 to 1942 saw the release of a trove of classic films that continue to captivate viewers to this day:

Casablanca
Citizen Kane
Destry Rides Again
Gone with the Wind
Goodbye, Mr. Chips
The Maltese Falcon
Mr. Smith Goes to Washington
Ninotchka
Rebecca
The Rules of the Game (La règle du jeu)
The Wizard of Oz
Young Mr. Lincoln

Citizen Kane changed the medium. It set new expectations for cinematic storytelling. Its director? Orson Welles, the same boy wonder who created a national panic with his radio play.

Americans went to the movies in record numbers each week. But things change. Television landed in living rooms, so many moviegoers landed on the couch. Today, not as many Americans go to the movies as they did back then, but more of the world goes. Hence, Hollywood's appetite for computer generated imagery (CGI) and animation spectacles. KA-BOOM! and SPLAT! are understood worldwide.

Pick up any issue of any magazine that covers entertainment, eavesdrop at a table where writers hang out, look at the original programming offered by not only the broadcast and cable networks, but also Netflix, Amazon and other streaming providers, and you will hear this consensus: we are in a golden age of television. It has never been better. Broadband and binge watching have changed the way stories are told. Audiences love long-form serialized storytelling. Kind of like what Dickens used to do. (Then again, many big game franchises have been providing long-form episodic storytelling for, well, a lot longer than Netflix has.)

Television as a storytelling medium did not begin with a golden age. Mom and Dad America did not unwrap their TV dinners and enjoy *Breaking Bad* or *The Sopranos*. For decades, many TV shows were essentially radio programs with pictures. (Many very early TV shows, like *Father Knows Best* and *The Adventures of Ozzie and Harriet*, started out as radio programs.) TV's current golden age—with its nuanced, cinematic storytelling—took close to seventy-five years to get here. For decades, television was the most underappreciated and most often disparaged medium (besides comic books). Theater critic John Mason Brown famously called TV "chewing gum for the eyes."[5] It was unfashionable in smart circles to declare that you might actually enjoy watching television. Does that attitude seem familiar to those of us who love video games?

THE GOLDEN AGE OF GAMES?

We've come a long way from the bouncing ball that was *Pong*. We are now in a golden age of video game storytelling. Thankfully, the technology

5   1955 June 6, Time, Radio: Conversation Piece, Time Inc., New York. (Accessed time.com on September 12 2013; Online Time Magazine Archive)

has plateaued in recent years. In the last generation of high-def game consoles, you could see the nose hair growing out of the nostrils of the zombies that were about to kill you. In the current "next generation," you can see individually animated legs on the mites on the nose hairs of the zombies that are about to kill you. For most game players, the most meaningful technological advancements of the last decade have been innovative controllers (via touch screens, cameras, plastic guitars, and wiggle sticks), better networking and, by far, the portability and ease of use provided by both smartphones and their app stores.

What's been so exciting about this is that so many creators have been able to focus on making more immersive and emotionally compelling stories with better gameplay, rather than having to spend so much time learning how to render graphics on totally new platforms. *Half-Life, Halo, Assassin's Creed, Fallout 3, BioShock, Uncharted, Mass Effect, The Last of Us*—all these landmark story-driven franchises have players returning again and again to experience the next chapter in the story; to explore more deeply these compelling worlds.

Although they're not "playable movies," their graphics and sound are cinematic. Advances in motion capture and a thousand other bits of technology allow more realism and beauty. The worlds and story lines have attracted A-list Hollywood talent. Music tracks are no longer the ping-ping-ping of an 8-bit chip but sweeping symphonic scores. World building and mythology are unparalleled. What was the norm for the video game industry now has become a key point in every story conference for movies and television. The creators and narrative designers of these games—Ken Levine (*BioShock*), Susan O'Connor (*Tomb Raider*), David Cage (*Heavy Rain*) and many others—are treated like rock stars at game conferences.

Agents, managers, and writers talk about how a writer in today's world should know how to write it all: movies, novels, plays, articles, and "webisodes." Even video games.

HOLLYWOOD CALLING!

Film and television industry executives have long been fascinated by video games. But, like many grown-ups, they've had a very hard time understanding them. But if there's one thing blockbuster movies *and* games have in common, it's that their creators and distributors are always pursuing *The Big Idea.*

Hollywood loves The Big Idea. The high-concept one-liner. The story that gets butts in movie seats. The tantalizing "What If?" question that people pay you to answer. The IP that can feed the fans' insatiable appetite for sequels and spin-offs (and book tie-ins and toys and T-shirts). Every big media company wants nothing more than a franchise like *Star Wars,* in which the slightest announcement of new information or release of a new trailer can fill the halls at comic conventions and might even crash Twitter.

The appeal is twofold: for creators and fans, it's about the fun of exploring an exciting world and getting to know fascinating characters; for the suits, it's about the *money!* As Gus Grissom (actor Fred Ward) says in *The Right Stuff,* "No bucks, no Buck Rogers."

The first modern American transmedia franchise was, arguably, *The Wizard of Oz* (and we don't mean the beloved 1939 MGM film—that came almost four decades later). L. Frank Baum wrote *The Wonderful Wizard of Oz* in 1900. The book was a best-seller for years, and Baum wrote thirteen more novels based in the "merry old land of Oz." He then brought the franchise to the stage as a musical play, which had a successful run on Broadway and toured the United States. In 1914 he expanded into movies with a series of silent films produced by his own Oz Film Manufacturing Company.[6] There were spin-offs and merchandise (both licensed and unlicensed) for nearly *forty years* before audiences ever got to see Judy Garland wear her sequined ruby slippers.

All these journeys to Oz across multiple media made Baum a fortune. (He later *lost* a fortune, but that's a different story.) Audiences bought his books and tickets to his shows because they already knew of Oz and its characters, but wanted to know more. It was much easier for Baum to sell a new Oz-based book—for which there was an existing audience—than it was for him to sell a new book set in a different world. (He tried

---

6   Baum, L. Frank. *The Wonderful Wizard of Oz.* Oxford University Press, 2008.

many times with non-Oz stories.) The film studio and game publisher marketing executives call this "pre-awareness," and it's the Holy Grail they're always pursuing.

Those pre-aware movie audiences love being taken to explore new locations within their favorite worlds, going on new emotional journeys with their favorite characters. The dramatic theory (according to Aristotle—more on him later) is that the audience empathically bonds with the main character, and as that *protagonist* changes, the audience comes to experience emotional change, or *catharsis*.

And all this happens when they are sitting—passively—in their movie seats. But we're not here to discuss *passive* entertainment; this book is about *interactive* entertainment.

WHY "SLAY THE DRAGON"?

With video games, players are in the driver's seat (sometimes literally, if it's a racing game like *Gran Turismo*). They are immersed—emotionally and physically—in the game. A hero in a movie might need to rescue the princess by slaying the big dragon, and we in the movie audience want to SEE him do it. But in a game, we the players want to slay the dragon and rescue the princess (or prince) through the vessel of the *player character* (PC). We also want plenty to do and see along the way. We're players; we want to play.

One of the axioms of dramatic writing is that *action is character*. If we see a character doing something, it defines who they are. But in video games, we're the ones driving the PC's actions. We're helping to define (and become) the character we control on the screen. These game *mechanics* are what the player gets to do in the game: Run. Jump. Shoot. Explore. Collect. Solve. Beat the Boss. *Be* the Boss. (More on all this later). They are motivated by story and quests and goals to pound the joystick, press X, Y. To lean forward and live in the story as the character would.

In the past, this was the most humbling thing for game writers to learn. Players are often not as interested in what happens in the story *you* have authored as they are in what happens in the story *they* are authoring themselves by playing the game. You, the writer, have to learn to tell your story through the lens of PLAYER ACTION. If the player cannot succeed, the character does not succeed. But the times have changed: players and audiences want deeper content and characters they can connect to. Why do we see gamers jumping back to Liberty City any chance they get?

In his groundbreaking book on Hollywood screenwriting, *Save the Cat*, the late Blake Snyder showed us how important it is for us in the movie audience to invest emotionally in the hero. He called those scenes that make us begin to root for the movie hero the *"Save the Cat* scenes." Video games have a very similar but more active principle: The players have to invest emotionally in the journey you've laid out for them.

The player wants to *slay the dragon*.

This is what the player cares about. The story has to involve the player. The player has to want to do and see cool things in the game world.

The game mechanics (such as dragon slaying) should enhance the story, and vice versa. They have to work in concert. We'll guide you in the coming pages so you understand how to tell your story through the gameplay in an integrated fashion. Gameplay is like action scenes in movies. They have to be organic to the story line for the audience to suspend disbelief and enjoy the ride. The best games accomplish this fine alchemy between narrative and gameplay so that one enhances and reinforces the other (think of the big mid-game twist in *BioShock*). Your quest, outlined in the chapters to come, is to master that alchemy.

MEET YOUR QUEST GIVERS: BOB & KEITH

In video games, NPCs are the *non-player characters* who often guide the PC through the world. These digital sidekicks hand out missions and information to the PC. They are the quest givers, the rule enforcers, the explainers. (Think of Cortana, the Master Chief's AI sidekick in *Halo*.) You know them in game worlds as mentors, vendors, barkeeps, passersby, teachers, and trainers. We are going to be your quest givers. We're excited to explore with you this complex, awe-inspiring world of video game narrative.

We are not going to steal your virtual loot and sell it on eBay (though one of us knows how).

Our story begins in a 1920s apartment complex on Orange Grove Avenue in the heart of Los Angeles. If the story has a title, it's *Aristotle vs. Mario*. It's a branching narrative (which is something we'll discuss later on when we talk about structure).

Bob and Keith had both recently graduated with master's degrees from top film schools—the University of Southern California and New York University, respectively. (The) found themselves living two doors from each other, and became friends over Ethiopian food on Fairfax Avenue, too many Oki-Dogs, the L.A. Riots, and drives down to the San Diego Comic-Con (back when you could still find parking).

Keith's path took him on the road to Hollywood. He co-wrote feature film scripts with his wife Juliet and was a working screenwriter for years.

Bob went to work in the video game business. He started at the bottom as game tester (think production assistant, mailroom clerk, or script reader). Bob quickly worked his way up the video game ladder, moving into product development and then becoming a studio director, serving as executive producer on dozens of games.

Bob spent hours playing all kinds of games, and way too much *World of Warcraft*. Keith would get schooled in *Halo* by his nephews. They continued to be friends, have dinners, go down to Comic-Con with professional passes, read comic books, and talk movies and games.

But even though they thought they were on divergent paths, their two worlds were gradually coming together. Xboxes and PlayStations were being marketed to adults, not just teens and parents. Kids who grew up playing video games were now working in the film business as writers, directors, and visual effects artists.

One year Bob took Keith to the Electronic Entertainment Expo (E3) at the Los Angeles Convention Center. (Think of it as the Cannes Film Festival for the video game industry.) It was Keith's very first time, and he felt like Luke walking into the cantina at Mos Eisley, but with less danger and fewer loppings. Way more lightsabers, though.

Keith saw a giant world of entertainment and exciting story lines enjoyed by millions of people. The crowds were huge, rushing between gigantic booths with stadium-sized screens set up by the game publishers and hardware makers: Activision. Ubisoft. Electronic Arts. Square-Enix. Xbox. PlayStation. Nintendo. The booths were lavishly designed, with characters from the games walking about for photo ops. The giant screens played the trailers for these games on continuous loop, their orchestral soundtracks booming throughout the halls: *Mass Effect, Assassin's Creed, Dragon Age, Final Fantasy.*

These games looked and felt like movies! The quality of the content was seductive. The computer animation was as good as watching the *Lord of the Rings* trilogy. But more importantly, the stories that were up on the screen were inviting, begging to be seen. Film and games are no longer distant cousins, they are blood brothers. The South by Southwest (SXSW) Festival focuses on music, film, and games. The 2013 Tribeca Film Festival debuted footage from a game called *Beyond: Two Souls* "starring" Ellen Page and Willem Dafoe. Kevin Spacey (*House of Cards'* Frank Underwood) plays the villain in a recent *Call of Duty*. Academy Award-winning composer Hans Zimmer wrote the music for *Call of Duty: Modern Warfare 2*.

The worlds have collided and the landscape of entertainment is bigger and teeming with possibilities. (Side note: the last time Bob and Keith went to E3, they accidentally wound up at a bar in the nearby Hotel Figueroa having cupcakes and beer with an adult film star, who was pitching her own game project. Our point is: everybody is getting into video games!)

Sure, movies have influenced games. *Uncharted* is an interactive Indiana Jones. *Tomb Raider* is a female Indiana Jones. In *Minecraft*, you are Indiana Jones.

But every relationship works two ways. Video games have also been influencing movies and books and television. Are we the only ones who thought the levels of the mind portrayed in *Inception* played out like video game levels?

The first blockbuster mainstream CD-ROM game was the classic *Myst*, about an island that contains lots of mysteries. Does that premise seem familiar to modern TV audiences? Here's what *Lost* co-creator

Damon Lindelof had to say about the similarities:

> For me certainly, the big game-changer was *Myst*. There's a lot of
> that feeling in *Lost*. What made it so compelling was also what made
> it so challenging. No one told you what the rules were. You just had
> to walk around and explore these environments and gradually a story
> was told. And *Lost* is the same way.[7]

Booker Prize-winning novelist Sir Salman Rushdie used video games as a form of escapism during his years of hiding from Ayatollah Khomeini's *fatwa*. He has said he is quite fond of Mario. Video game structure has influenced his storytelling. His novel *Luka and the Fire of Life* contains a main character, "Super Luka," who is given 999 lives and has to pass through a number of "levels" to steal the fire of life and use it to wake his father from a coma. He remarked how non-linear narrative is fascinating for him to explore. "I think that really interests me as a storyteller," he said, "to tell the story sideways."[8]

SCREENWRITER MEETS GAME PRODUCER, FIGHT BREAKS OUT

Remember we said our story was branching? Let's return to it. Keith continued to work as a film and television writer, but he always kept one eye open a little wider on what was happening in video games. Bob went on to executive produce more games. He was working on a game that had been mechanic-driven and was based on a toy company's IP. The game world, though, seemed a little thin.

"I need a writer," he said to Keith in the food court of the L.A. Convention Center. They were taking a break from a comic book show.

"For what?" Keith asked, his feet still aching from walking the picket lines for the then-in-progress Writers Guild strike.

---

7 http://entertainment.time.com/2007/03/19/lyst_cuse_and_lindelof_on_lost_1/ In the same article, he says "we have a lot of gamers on our writing staff."

8 http://www.theverge.com/2012/10/10/3482926/salman-rushdie-video-game-escapism-hiding

"A game I'm producing. If you want to audition for it, I need you to write some barks for the NPCs."

"Barks?" "NPCs?" Bob was speaking a language different from what Keith was used to hearing. (It's a language we'll teach you in the coming pages.) Keith asked a few questions, figured it out, wrote some barks and auditioned for the job of "narrative designer," which is game-speak for "staff writer." Then Keith went to work for Bob at a toy company writing video games.

Although they'd written and commented on each other's work for years, this was the first time they worked together professionally. They got along very well, except when they would argue about the role that story should play in the game.

"It's not a movie!"

"The character needs more of an arc!"

"Agency?!? What the heck is *that*?"

"The audience has to care! They have to be involved!"

"They're *players*, not an audience!"

It was story points vs. game mechanics. It was Aristotle vs. Mario; drama vs. fun. They would spend hours discussing dramatic structure of movies and television and video games. What was the same? What was different? It was an ongoing education, from which they decided to create a course in game writing offered through the prestigious Writers' Program at UCLA Extension.

Their very first class was a day-long seminar. They had no idea who, if anyone, would show up. It was on a sunny 75-degree Sunday in Westwood. Who'd want to sit in a room with Bob and Keith and learn about story structure, game mechanics, and barks?

But the classroom was packed. Every seat was taken. There were people who worked in game design and community management; there were screenwriters; there were aspiring game designers; and, most surprisingly, an A-list actress/producer and her husband/producing partner, himself a working TV actor. During a break Keith asked her, "Why are you taking this class?" She said it was because she knew this was an emerging arena for storytellers and as a producer she wanted to know more.

Keith and Bob went on to expand the class to a full-semester course in the Writers' Program at UCLA. Keith then moved east and now teaches the class at Syracuse University. Bob has taken the class to new heights, both teaching it online internationally and incorporating it into game production courses he creates at other schools.

They have seen their students enter the game industry armed with a deep understanding of how story works for games.

This is our goal for you, the reader of this book. To level up your abilities as a writer.

WHO NEEDS THIS BOOK?

We're convinced that in order for them to succeed, today's screenwriters *must* understand the interactive medium.

Many film directors working today openly acknowledge the influence video games have on their work. Listen to director Joe Cornish, discussing his movie *Attack the Block*:

> "The monsters were kind of inspired by a SNES game called *Another World,* which was one of the first games to use motion capture," Cornish said. "It had some terrific creatures that were made out of silhouettes." The idea of staging *Attack the Block*'s events in a single location was something else that, Cornish maintains, came from the realm of video games. It was, he said, a "unified space"—something commonly seen in first-person shooters.[9]

Dan Trachtenberg directed an original short film based on the video game *Portal*. It went viral, logging more than fifteen million views.[10] He is now attached to direct the movie version of the comic book *Y: The Last Man* written by Brian K. Vaughn, a comic book writer and producer on *Lost*.

---

9 http://www.denofgeek.us/movies/18632/the-growing-influence-of-videogames-on-movies
10 http://youtu.be/4drucg1A6Xk

Warner Bros. scored a huge hit with *The Lego Movie*. Audiences have been playing with Lego for years. But in all the reviews (which were glowing) and discussions of the film's success, we noticed a complete lack of love for the Lego games. For years, people have been living in Lego worlds, not just with the toy bricks, but with the funny animated adventures that go along with playing any of the Lego games, including *Lego Indiana Jones*, *Lego Star Wars*, and *Lego Batman*. It's the Lego games of the last 10 years, made by English developer Traveller's Tales, which inspired *The Lego Movie*'s comic sensibility. The Lego movie only broke new ground in movie theaters. There was an audience of millions already familiar with that world. We were disappointed that film reviewers didn't acknowledge this.

Seizing on the success of the Lego movie, it's no wonder Warner Bros. has put *Minecraft* into accelerated development as a feature film franchise. To millions of people around the world it's already a franchise! A movie would be icing on a very big cake that has already been baked. (BTW, the creator of *Minecraft* was able to purchase a $70 million home in Los Angeles. We guess you need a pretty big kitchen for that pretty big cake.)

Remember those story pitches that started this chapter? As we write this, they are all in development as motion pictures. Michael "Magneto" Fassbender is attached to star in *Assassin's Creed*. Ridley Scott's company is developing the *Halo* feature film. Although, as of this writing, it's stuck in "development hell," we fully expect to be on line the first day for the *BioShock* movie.

Assassin's Creed publisher Ubisoft has been compared to the next Marvel for raising money to develop its own properties for the big screen, including two games based on Tom Clancy novels-turned-game franchises: *Splinter Cell* (with Tom Hardy attached) and *Ghost Recon*.[11]

Games are not just about games anymore. The worlds are colliding. Swirling around you. It can be very confusing. We're here to clear up the differences, to bridge the similarities, and to get you thinking about that alchemy!

---

11 http://screenrant.com/video-game-movies-future/

We hope you find the ideas and exercises within to be a worthy quest. We wrote this book for you, if you are:

- a writer who wants to explore interactive storytelling,
- a writer who wants to understand the role of story in the game development process,
- a game writer (or gameplay designer) who wants to make your work more integrated and emotionally resonant with gameplay (and vice versa); or
- a passionate fan of story-driven video games.

At the end of each chapter are some Dragon Exercises. We encourage you to do them. Let us be your quest givers here to take you through world-building, character creation, branching narratives, and game mechanics (among many other topics).

It's time to begin your journey.

It's time to *slay the dragon*!

HOW TO USE THIS BOOK (PRESS X TO SKIP)

Movies (and television) and video games; video games and movies. This book is a bridge between those two types of media. Let's call them *linear narrative* and *interactive narrative*.

You may be very familiar with the material on linear narrative: character, conflicts, and all the other tenets of drama. But you might not know anything about game mechanics and gameplay. Or, you may be an avid game player—or game creator—who is familiar with gameplay but might not know about story structure. With that in mind, we have laid out some "choose-your-own-adventure" options to help guide you through the book. As much as we hate to skip over cut scenes, sometimes it happens. So we are providing you with a SKIP button here.

If You Are a Writer and Know a Little about Games

Most of this book is going to be new to you. Sure, you will be tempted to skip over story and jump right to gameplay. But you want to make sure you read the story material also, for it is wildly different in interactive narrative.

Must-read chapters: *all of them!*

If You Are a Game Developer and Know a Little about Story

For a game dev, a chapter like "What's in a Game?" may seem like a boot camp tutorial. So skip it. And you can probably skip over game mechanics. But don't pass up story, or characters. Even level design has something to offer on how it applies to what keeps viewers in their seats—engaging content.

Must-read chapters:
2. Do Games Need Stories?
3. Aristotle vs. Mario
4. The No-Act-Fits-All Structure of Video Games
5. Writing a Great Playable Character
6. Who Am I When I Play? Gameplay as Method Acting
8. The Hero of a Thousand Levels
9. Building Your World with the Narrative Design Toolbox
12. What Happens Next?

If You Are a Film Producer or Creative Exec
Looking for the Next Big Crossover IP

Everyone wants to be that genius at the studio who makes the video game movie (or TV show) work. So far it hasn't. Why is that? We think you should read through the entire book to make your job easier. Bridge the two worlds together. You are not looking to break into the video game business, so you will probably skip most of the exercises as well.

Must-read chapters:
1. What's in a Game?
2. Do Games Need Stories?
3. Aristotle vs. Mario
4. The No-Act-Fits-All Structure of Video Games
5. Writing a Great Playable Character
6. Who Am I When I Play? Gameplay as Method Acting
7. Game Design Basics for Writers
8. The Hero of a Thousand Levels
12. What Happens Next?

If You Teach and Use this as a Textbook

Everything in this book has been beta-tested in our classrooms. We have structured the book so you can use it to map out your semester. Each chapter contains exercises and projects that we have workshopped with our own students with great success. Our students have gone on to work in the video game field as writers, producers, testers, and even journalists.

Must-read chapters: *all of them!*

If You Are a Hobbyist and Want to Make Your Own Game

Read it all the way through from beginning to the end. (And don't forget the exercises!)

—

Playing to Learn

AT THE END of each chapter we've suggested some exercises for you to do. This is not homework. This is fun. This is brainstorming, or getting your brain ready to be stormed with your great game idea(s).

1 START YOUR GAME JOURNAL

Games are meant to be played. Funny how simple that seems, but it is the truth. But now when you play a game, we want you to play with a more analytical eye. Start a Game Journal, and fill it with your reflections on and impressions of every game you play, good or bad. Record your thoughts during or shortly after the game.

2 PLAY A BOARD GAME

For your first entry, we want you to play a board game. But not a game that's sitting in the basement of Mom's house, or in your closet. Play a *new* board game—one that you've never played before.

Board games have enjoyed a renaissance over the last decade or so. Actor Wil Wheaton (*Star Trek: The Next Generation*) hosts a web series called "Table Top," which features celebrities and game industry veterans playing new board games.

But why do you need to play a board game?

The Writer will probably be the player who loves to read the backstory that might come with the instructions; or really like the world as described on the back of the box. But board games are a great way for writers to start thinking about game design. As Writers play board games, they should ask: What are the rules? What are the obstacles? Are there rewards and achievements? Setbacks? How is the game structured? This is not a book about balancing gameplay based on statistics and math. It's a book on game story. But as Writers will soon learn, story and gameplay go together. How does the gameplay in the board game reflect its story or world?

The Gamer probably knows all about the gameplay. He or she will be able to see the framework of the game the way a screenwriter would see story structure. So the Gamer needs to play a new board game and concentrate on the story—the world—of the game. Who are the characters? How are they represented? What is the story line? What is the goal of the characters, and is that different from the goal(s) of the players? How is the world of the game conveyed to the player?

Play a game and in one page describe the world of the story, the plot, and the game play. Record your impressions in your Game Journal.

Some board games that are well worth playing if you haven't tried them are:

Battlestar Galactica
King of New York
Myth
Quantum
Puerto Rico
Settlers of Catan
Sheriff of Nottingham
Ticket to Ride

If you're still stumped as to what to try, there are plenty of great suggestions at www.boardgamegeek.com.

3 PLAY A VIDEO GAME

(We realize this may be stunningly obvious.)

Way too many games; way too little time. Keith tells his screenwriting students to watch all of the films on the American Film Institute's list of the "100 Greatest American Films of All Time." Well, aspiring game writers need to do the same sort of thing. However, there is no definitive list of the top 100 games, although many lists agree on many great games. Many game magazines and web sites publish such lists periodically. But you as a writer should focus on the more story-driven games. (*Pong* is, after all, simply *Pong*.) Although many classic games have been "remastered" for play on modern systems ranging from PCs to smartphones, not every old game ages well.

Play games that have been recognized in the last five years or so for their engaging stories or immersive worlds. Play games on a computer, on a console, on a smartphone or tablet. Play indie games. Download and play trial and demo versions. Play games in various game genres to get the feel of how they work. Play a sports game like *FIFA* or *NBA 2K*. (Yes, these do have stories.)

Play best-sellers, critics' darlings, and award winners. Although the games industry does not yet have its "Academy Awards," it's worth paying attention to any such list. Some of the story-driven nominees and winners of The Game Awards 2014 included:

Bravely Default
Broken Age: Act I
Divinity
Dragon Age: Inquisition
Middle-earth: Shadow of Mordor
South Park: The Stick of Truth
The Vanishing of Ethan Carter
The Walking Dead, Season Two
The Wolf Among Us
This War of Mine
Valiant Hearts: The Great War
Wolfenstein: The New Order

We also recommend in our classes games from the following list, in which we find the narrative, characters, or world very compelling, and gameplay organic to the story line. They are also interactive narratives that we feel make the best use of the tools of video game writing.

Assassin's Creed franchise
Beyond Good & Evil
BioShock
BioShock Infinite
Braid
Brothers: A Tale of Two Sons
Deus Ex franchise
Fallout
Fallout 3
Final Fantasy VII
God of War
Half-Life
Halo franchise
Heavy Rain
Ico
Journey
The Last of Us
Mass Effect franchise
Portal
Portal 2
The Stanley Parable

(Please don't freak out if your favorite game isn't on the list. This is a short list, and is by no means definitive. We only present it here as a jumping-off point for you to begin to explore story-driven games.)

Play a game and in one page describe the world, the plot, and the gameplay. Record your impressions in your Game Journal.

CHAPTER 01

WHAT'S IN A GAME?

A GAME IS NOT A MOVIE, and a movie is not a game.

No one decides to go out for the evening to watch a game; and we can't imagine a scenario where friends text each other: SUP? U WANNA PLAY A MOVIE?

It makes no sense. How can you play a movie? You watch a movie. How do you see a game? You play a game. (Although Amazon's billion dollar purchase of Twitch.tv is the latest evidence that video games are becoming something you *watch* as well—a spectator sport.[12])

Games and movies are two distinct media. Filmed entertainment (movies, TV, scripted Internet videos—anything written for a screen) and video games are at once incredibly similar and totally different. But as these two storytelling platforms align more and more, certain conventions from the one have begun to influence the other. Two of the best recent video game movies were not based on actual video games. *Edge of Tomorrow* and *Snowpiercer* are both movies that feature video game tropes which may or may not be recognizable to the non-game-playing audience.

So what exactly do we mean by "video game"?

WHAT WE TALK ABOUT WHEN WE TALK ABOUT GAMES

Let's get the easy part out of the way: "Video" means, effectively, "played on a screen using a computer." That computer may be in your mobile phone, your game console, or your laptop. But we like to use "video games"

---

12 http://www.forbes.com/sites/ryanmac/2014/08/25/amazon-pounces-on-twitch-after-google-balks-due-to-antitrust-concerns/

to cover all computer games. Fair? Good. We'll generally be talking about digital (computer) games throughout the book. We have mad respect for the writing and world building that goes into so many popular "analog" (table-top) games, but, frankly, Bob still hasn't learned to play *Settlers of Catan*, so we'll usually be talking about video games. But not always.

The hard part—defining "game"—is a lot harder, especially since the ludologists got involved. (Ludology is the academic study of games and gameplay.) We are in a very evolving period of time as a debate rages about what exactly is a game.

Legendary designer Sid *"Civilization"* Meier said that "games are a series of interesting decisions."[13]

Respected ludologist Jesper Juul said that a "game is a rule-based system with a variable and quantifiable outcome, where different outcomes are assigned different values, the player exerts effort in order to influence the outcome, the player feels emotionally attached to the outcome, and the consequences of the activity are negotiable."[14]

Iconoclastic indie developer and critic Anna Anthropy wrote that a game is defined as "an experience created by rules."[15]

For our purposes, we like Ms. Anthropy's definition the best, as it's the least limiting, most versatile, and shortest.

But what are some of the core aspects of a game? And are any of these characteristics also found in other storytelling media like films or television?

Goals and Obstacles

Games have goals. Classic board games expressed this as "The Object of the Game" printed at the top of the instructions. In order to make those goals challenging, games have obstacles. From a pawn blocking a pawn

---

13 http://www.gamasutra.com/view/news/164869/GDC_2012_Sid_Meier_on_how_to_see_games_as_sets_of_interesting_decisions.php

14 Juul, Jesper. 2005. *Half-Real: Video Games between Real Rules and Fictional Worlds.* Ebook. 1st ed. Cambridge, MA: MIT Press, loc 400.

15 Anthropy, Anna. 2012. *Rise of the Videogame Zinesters: How Freaks, Normals, Amateurs, Artists, Dreamers, Dropouts, Queers, Housewives, and People Like You Are Taking Back an Art Form.* Ebook. 1st ed. New York, NY: Seven Stories Press., Loc. 939.

in a game of chess to Jail in *Monopoly* or backtracking down a chute in *Chutes and Ladders*, there will always be obstacles to impede the progress of the player.

Drama in any form must have obstacles and conflict. If Odysseus had used Google Maps, the *Odyssey* would have been a lot shorter and way less interesting.

Characters

"I want to be the top hat!" Have you ever heard this? It can happen any time a group sits down to play *Monopoly*. Games often have characters that are "acted" by the players during the gameplay. Remember *Clue*? We humans have a way of identifying with (and as) other people (real or fictional), animals, and plants (see *Plants vs. Zombies*)—even inanimate objects, like *Monopoly*'s top hat. Even colors. Growing up, Bob always wanted to play as black in checkers. He thought black was smarter and cooler than red or white.

The play has a character (or "avatar") who is—for the player—the protagonist of the story. There must also be antagonists. These can be other players, or computer controlled villains—obstacles that move and act and have cool dialogue.

Settings (or the Game World)

When you sit down to play a game, the game maker provides the dramatic context. The world. The setup. Building the world is the first step to creating an immersive experience for the player. Where does the game take place? The historic Atlantic City of *Monopoly*? The imaginary island of Catan? The nineteenth century United States of *Ticket to Ride*? Even such "simple" board games as *Stratego*, *Battleship*, and *Risk* show us a world—namely, combat in the field, at sea, and on a global scale. (By the way, where the heck did the aliens in the *Battleship* movie come from? They weren't in our game box!)

Competition

Competition is a huge component of gameplay. Players compete against each other, or the game, or both, to win. In single-player video games, players play against the game system, but they may also be playing against the entire world when it comes to online leaderboards and achievements. Scripted drama consists largely of us watching a "competition" and rooting for the "good guy," be they Othello, Atticus Finch, or Katniss Everdeen.

And, perhaps most importantly:

Rules

Games have rules. It's the first thing participants discuss when starting a game. Someone will explain the rules. How to move. What the cards mean. How to win.

Movies and TV shows also have rules. Drama has rules. Characters must be motivated. Clues must be planted. Conflict must be resolved somehow. When stories deviate from these rules, we often find them unsettling, unsatisfying, or a Lars von Trier film.

Rules matter in games. Yes, there are some games where you *play without rules.* These are games you might have played at the playground in a sandbox as a kid. (Remember that word: sandbox.) Peek-a-Boo. Ring Around the Roses. Make-believe games like House or Dinosaurs. But on the same playground you might have kids playing games where they have to **play with rules.** Hide and Seek. Duck, Duck, Goose. Four Square (the ball game, not the app). All sports and card games.

And of course, board games.

So what is a rule? Think of it like an "if-then" statement. *If* I do or accomplish this, *then* this other thing will happen. It could be a reward or a setback. Simply put, when playing a *Call of Duty* or a *Battlefield:*

> *If* I fall on a grenade, *then* I will die.

At some point during a board game, players might have to refer to the rule book or instruction manual. Computers are awesome because they automate the rules, making them close to invisible. The computer rolls the dice, does the math (physics and calculus) instantly, keeps score, and referees. The computer tracks changes in the game's state (positions, statistics, achievements, etc.). Imagine having someone at the table on game night doing all that. In so many games, the computer is your Dungeon Master, without the sarcasm or the onion-ring breath. Because the computer is running the game, the player can stay immersed in the world of the game. Finally, when it's time for more of the story, the computer plays that content flawlessly, every time.

However, games are not only about the experience created by the rule systems. They're about the story also. Stories have rules as well. Just think of all the rules associated with opening the lost Ark, or using the Force? Or how someone can awaken from a dream in *Inception*. Players (and characters) make choices that affect outcomes, and those outcomes affect further choices the player can make. It's a feedback loop: Rules create consequences. Consequences create feelings. Those feelings affect the player's next actions, and those actions are again judged by the rules. And so on, tens of thousands of times per play session.

Think about the emotions you feel when you are playing a game and have to GO DIRECTLY TO JAIL. Or when you finally solve the puzzle that's been thwarting your progress. Or when you find that one hidden item that will complete your quest. Our goal as game writers is to use those feelings to deepen the narrative experience for the player. This is the storytelling alchemy that games can possess—a combination of gameplay and narrative.

We'll explore story further in the next chapter, but for now, let's say that a story is a **journey of emotion**. If that's true, and we feel it is, then it's useful to think of a game as a **journey of action**.

A GAME IS A JOURNEY OF ACTION

What action? Everything: the action the player takes, the resulting action that the game system (or an opposing player) takes, then the resulting subsequent actions that the players take, etc.

Game mechanics are the actions that a player can take in a game. They are the "verbs" of the game. Gameplay designers are always thinking about what the players can do in a level, just as screenwriters are always thinking about what the characters are doing in a scene. What makes sense? What's challenging? What's too easy or too boring?

Here's a brutally incomplete list of some common game mechanics, with some example games. Think about games that you've played recently, or your favorites. Which mechanics do you recognize from this list? Which are missing?

Moving

This can cover a lot, like **running** at a fixed speed (*Temple Run, Canabalt*) or **accelerating** and **decelerating**, often while **steering** (*Pole Position, Project Gotham Racing*). You might be **jumping** (*Super Mario Bros.*) and **ducking** (*Super Mario Bros. 3*) to avoid obstacles or to reach platforms. You can move to pursue or to avoid, **fleeing** enemies (*Pac-Man*) or **chasing** them (powered-up *Pac-Man*).

Exploring

This might be **seeking** a hidden switch in a room (*Myst, The Room*) or a more general **exploring** of a level or a world to discover its wonders (*World of Warcraft*). You could be **collecting** things (*Pokémon, Lego Star Wars*) or **gathering** resources (*Minecraft*). If someone is searching for you, then perhaps you should think about **hiding** (*Metal Gear Solid*).

Planning

This is a broad one, as it can include **managing** (*SimCity, Roller Coaster Tycoon*), **strategizing** (*Civilization, Rise of Nations*), or simply **buying** and **selling** (*The Sims*, franchise mode in *Madden*). You may be **choosing** which weapon or power-up to use (*Angry Birds, Mario Kart*), **arranging** gems or other things (*Bejeweled, Puzzle Quest*), or **allocating** cards in your deck or points to your character (*Magic: The Gathering* or *Mass Effect*).

Fighting

This can include **attacking** and **defending** in individual hand-to-hand combat (*Street Fighter, Tekken*), on the squad level (*Final Fantasy Tactics*) or as a clash of armies (*StarCraft*, the *Total War* series). Although some games feature intimate **stabbing**, both more secretive (*Assassin's Creed*) and less (*Chivalry: Medieval Warfare*), by far the most popular form of combat in video games is **shooting**. Whether the shooting is done from a side view (*R-Type*), a top-down view (*Asteroids*), an over-the shoulder view (*Gears of War*), or a first-person view (*Quake, Unreal, Halo* and so many others), players love to point at a target, press a button, and let the simulated physics fall where they may.

Timing

This is another broad one, as it can include **volleying** the ball in *Pong* or *Breakout*, **matching** your steps or strums to the beats in *Dance Dance Revolution* or *Guitar Hero*, or **swinging** your club in *Hot Shots Golf*.

We warned you this list is brutally short. What have we missed? We'll dig deeper into this in Chapter 07: Game Design Basics for Writers.

Remember that many games, and very many story games, tend to combine several mechanics, either simultaneously or in phases. In the *Grand Theft Auto* games you race sometimes, you shoot sometimes, and sometimes you shoot while racing. In *Sid Meier's Pirates!* you sword fight, sail, and trade, amongst other piratey activities.

Understanding a game's mechanics is crucial to where it is placed, both on the retail shelf and in the minds of game players, because historically, that's how we think of game genres.

GAME GENRE VS. STORY GENRE

Stories are journeys of emotion. We tend to group movies and television—along with novels and plays—by the emotions they evoke (comedy, horror, romance, etc.).

Games are journeys of action, however. We tend to group games by their core mechanics (racing, shooting, role-playing, etc.). Players who enjoy a certain mechanic tend to look for other games with the same mechanics they enjoy, just as people who enjoy mystery novels look for more mysteries to read. That's why retailers often put *Halo* and *Call of Duty* on the same shelf. Even though one is a space opera and the other is an urban combat simulator, they share the same core mechanic: point-and-click shooting. But just because we group games by their mechanics doesn't mean that story isn't important to our enjoyment of games. The story should complement the mechanics of the genre and vice versa. It all comes together during the development and production of the game. With that in mind, we want to touch on how video games are actually made.

HOW DO THEY MAKE GAMES? WHO'S THE DIRECTOR?

Movies have directors. They're the ultimate boss on a film set; they are responsible for managing all the creative and technical departments so that the hundreds of people who work on the film are executing toward bringing the director's coherent creative vision to the movie.

The movie-making process developed in Europe and America over a century ago, and its customs and practices—its industry culture—is very deeply rooted. It would be hard to imagine a film without a director, and we have a long tradition of genius-level *auteurs* (Welles, Hitchcock, Bergman, Fellini, Kubrick, . . .).

Games do not have directors, per se. They sometimes have creative directors, or design directors, or occasionally you'll see a "directed by" or "game director" credit on large projects or some Japanese games, but the term is rare. There may be a person (say, the "Director of Game Design") who owns the creative vision of the game, but he is always working with the producer (responsible for the schedule and budget) and the technical director (or lead programmer, responsible for the coding), as well as the other department heads (art, audio, marketing, live team, testing, community managers, etc.) to balance their creative vision against the other resources (Time! Money!) that are running short on the project.

The process of making computer games emerged four decades ago in Japan, America, and Europe, and each region's game development culture is a little different. In America, the game development process still often reflects the well-established process of "grown-up" software development—banking, medicine, aviation—that arose in the 1960s and '70s. There, the clients (represented by marketing) often dictated their needs or creative vision, which was mediated by a project manager, who then "managed" teams of programmers, who wrote the software. (If it seems "Dilbert"-y, it is.)

Fortunately, game development can be a lot more democratic, in the sense that managing the entire team (which is done by producers or project managers, not a director) relies a lot more on consensus building—and horse trading—than orders dictated through a megaphone by an auteur in a canvas chair. There is often a "blue sky" period very early on in the conception phase. No good (or bad) idea goes unexpressed.

Blue sky is the honeymoon period of creativity. Anything is possible. Creators meet, brainstorm, spitball. They might be producers, designers, and writers who work from this mantra: If we can have anything in the world in our game, what might it be? Blue sky starts the collaborative process and differs greatly from the screenplay-driven, authorial process of Hollywood. Sure, the creative producer of the game will reject most ideas—but the ideas will be heard.

There are, of course, a few video game auteurs who work like, and have fans like, film directors: Hideo Kojima (*Metal Gear Solid*), Sid Meier (*Civilization*), Will Wright (*SimCity*, *The Sims*), Tim Schafer (*Grim Fandango*), and Ken Levine (*BioShock*), among a few others. But they remain the exception rather than the rule.

WHERE DO GAME IDEAS COME FROM?

When Bob was working as a game tester at Mattel, he thought he had a great idea for a game: Mattel should resurrect its then moribund "Masters of the Universe" IP and make a hardcore action game aimed at the then 20- and 30-year-olds who grew up playing with He-Man and Skeletor. Because it was aimed at a mature audience, Bob envisioned the game as a gritty, noir take on He-Man. Skeletor had years ago conquered Castle Greyskull. He-Man had been stripped of his Sword of Power and had been banished to hard labor in a forgotten astro-mine. Bob pulled together an ad hoc group of artists and producers (who often doubled as gameplay designers) from the studio and pitched them his idea over lunch.

"We open up with three of He-Man's buddies huddled around

a campfire. They're leaderless, oppressed, and homeless. One starts to sing . . ." and then Bob launched into a song he'd written that would cover the action in the first cut scene.

"Wait a minute," a producer said. "Is this a *game* you're pitching? What do I get to do?"

"Well, fight your way out of the mines and re-take Castle Greyskull."

"Fine, that's the story—but what do I get to *do*?"

Bob had figured that details like gameplay could be sorted later. He was wrong.

His experience was typical for screen and fiction writers who move into game writing. It's a very sobering realization that you, the writer(s), are never the prime creator of a game. Fledgling game writers get told almost daily, "we can't do that," by producers or programmers. A simple idea like "let's make our hero swim!" can have a huge impact on the schedule and budget of a game, because implementing that suggestion would require the time and money involved to create entirely unanticipated models, textures, and animation trees. The sad irony is that for an interactive medium, it is often very difficult in video game development to adapt on the fly in the middle of a project.

That's the bad news. And it is also looking in the rear-view mirror. The good news is that more than ever, developers at every level need good writers to compete in the marketplace as the medium—and the audience—grows more sophisticated and discriminating. We are just beginning to unlock the potential of video games as a form of artistic self-expression.

Although game concepts traditionally have been driven by technology and game mechanics, this is changing. The idea for *The Last of Us* did not come from the mechanics. It came from the mind of the writer/ co-director Neil Druckmann. He wanted to develop a game version of the iconic zombie movie *Night of the Living Dead*. Unable to get the rights, he came up with his own—a mash-up of *Night of the Living Dead* and the classic PlayStation 2 game *Ico*.[16] Druckmann made the idea his

---

16 The Making of "The Last of Us" - Part 1: A Cop, A Mute Girl and Mankind, http://youtu. be/Fbpvzq-pfjc, retrieved January 20, 2015.

own, blending story and game mechanics in a way that resulted in a game-changing game.

THE NARRATIVE DESIGNER

The process of video game production suffers when a writer is brought in late to the project to assemble all the assets and make something that is cohesive. A narrative designer might be brought into the project early. On his blog *The Narrative Design Explorer,* "transmedia story designer and interactive design evangelist" Stephen Dinehart[17] put together one of the best job descriptions we've seen of the role and responsibilities of a narrative designer. He wrote that:

> The Narrative Designer will focus on ensuring that the key elements of the player experience associated with story and storytelling devices, script and speech are dynamic, exciting and compelling.

A job title has emerged recently that's often junior to narrative designer: content designer. But whatever it's called, we hope that you will one day soon be working for (running, perhaps?) the game developer of your choice.

But let's learn to crawl before we fly. Let's break things down all the way to their fundamentals.

Let's talk about story. See you in the next chapter.

---

17 http://narrativedesign.org/about/

Making A Game

1 WRITE YOUR OWN GAME

In this exercise, gameplay will be locked, and it's up to you to make the game as interesting as possible using only the tools of storytelling. The game is a simple dice race:

BOARD GAME

1. Two players
2. One six-sided die
3. Both players start on the same space (#1). Taking turns, each player rolls the die and moves their token one to six spaces around the board.

4. The first player to reach the end space (#32) wins!

As you've already figured out, this is the most boring gameplay possible. It's up to you and your imagination to bring the game to life by deciding what world the game takes place in, who the two players are, and what happens in each "scene" (space) as the players move toward the end of the game (and the story).

Don't leave any space blank!

The simplest method is to complete a matrix like this one:

SPACE	STORY CONTENT
1.	
2.	
3.	
4.	
etc.	

We have done this in class many times. We want storytellers to begin to use board games as a way of telling their stories. One student did an "extreme sports survival" game about a trip to climb Mount Everest. Five players climbed a mountain with gear and rations and were caught in a snowstorm and trapped. Will they make it? Play the game and find out. Each space brought you deeper into the world. The language and tone immersed the player in the world of extreme mountain climbing. It was complex but simple. You want to have a clear goal.

Remember, *don't change the rules*, or redesign the game board. You're writing on top of a game that has already been designed (professional game writers have to do this all the time). Save your urge to design gameplay for the next exercise.

2 TURN YOUR FAVORITE MOVIE INTO A BOARD GAME

This exercise is the opposite of the first one. Now you will focus on creating gameplay to reflect an existing story. Try it with your favorite classic movie. Why classic? Because chances are that your favorite recent movie is already a board game (and no fair turning *Battleship* or *Clue* back into board games).

Choose a classic film that falls outside the action/adventure genre: *Citizen Kane, Silence of the Lambs, When Harry Met Sally, Animal House, Dr. Strangelove, Dirty Dancing, The Breakfast Club* . . . How would you make such a movie into a board game? You can make it any type of game you want, but the simpler the better. We are not looking for you to make 3D printed character pieces with an elaborately designed game board.

DESIGN THE GAME BOARD

1. Create a simple board game using a game template. You can use the board game above or do an Internet search for "Board Game Templates" if you want more examples.
2. Choose a board. You now begin to see a structure. Do all this in pencil. Very rudimentary.
3. Write down your ideas. How do you see the game being played out? What is the objective of the game?
4. What are the mechanics? Dice? How many? Are there cards that need to be created and drawn?
5. How many players can play at one time? Is the game competitive or cooperative?

THE STORY OF THE GAME

1. How do the beats (plot points, story events) in the movie lead to the end of the game? Think of the pivotal scenes in the movie you have chosen. How can they be represented on the game board?
2. Do you need cards or branching paths to represent turning points in the story? How can you represent progress and setbacks? Does a setback put you back three spaces? Six? It's up to you.
3. Who are your characters? Let's say it's a hero vs. villain game. Will you have the good guy start in one direction around the board while the bad guy starts moving in the other direction? If

they land on the same space, will they fight? How do they fight? Do they roll dice? What are the results of that fight?

TEST THE GAME

1. Write down the rules.
2. Play the game. Test it. Have friends play it and watch them play. Record your observations in your Game Journal
3. Rewrite the rules.
4. Have more friends play it. Record more observations.

REFINE THE GAME

1. Redo and refine the artwork.
2. Rewrite the game rules and add a story introduction.
3. Rewrite the cards. Do they stay in a character's voice?

Think about how you can keep the spirit and the tone of the original movie. Does the voice you use on the cards match the voice of the movie? For example, if the game is *Silence of the Lambs,* do the cards read as if they were written by Hannibal Lecter? By Agent Clarice Starling? By Buffalo Bill?

CHAPTER 02

DO GAMES NEED STORIES?

"Let us now discuss the proper structure of the Plot, since this is the first and most important thing . . ." Aristotle. *Poetics.*

ARISTOTLE IS CONSIDERED to be the first story guru. He knew the importance of story structure to both the comprehension and enjoyment of the story, play, or poem. In *Poetics* he analyzed the method of creating plays and poems—the dominant storytelling forms of pre-Christian Greece—charting the role of the *protagonist* (main character) as his or her story unfolds in front of an audience. Aristotle probably never imagined a world where the audience of a play might become either the protagonists or the coauthors of the play. Yet this is what happens in video games and other forms of interactive storytelling.

STORY MATTERS

At this point, let's address and discard one of the stalest canards in game development: Stories don't matter to games. Story, narrative, setting, and world are as crucial to a video game as gameplay, character design, art direction, sound effects, or music. Try to imagine playing a game with no gameplay, character design, art direction, sound effects, or music. What would that be? Digital tic-tac-toe? Would you enjoy it? Would you play for very long? Would you tell your friends about it? As lifelong writers, we get a little impatient when we hear someone declare firmly that "games are not a storytelling medium."

Of *course* games can be a storytelling medium, just as books can be a storytelling medium. The fact that some books are phone directories doesn't negate *The Road, On The Road,* or *Oryx and Crake.* We game creators should stop thinking of our medium as being one monolithic, homogenous whole. We should also stop thinking as one monolithic, homogenous hive mind. Games tell stories—they just do so in ways that differ from linear media. A game player navigates what Juul calls "the half-real zone between the fiction and the rules."[18]

However, not all games are equally story-driven. Generally, story matters more in representational (more realistic) games than in presentational (more abstract) games.

Story Is Very Important . . .

In action/adventure game franchises (*Tomb Raider, Uncharted, God of War*), a compelling narrative is crucial to the gameplay. These games send their player characters into exciting and dangerous new worlds where they search for treasure, solve puzzles, and fight enemies. Players know at every turn what Lara Croft or Nathan Drake are after, and the narrative framework helps them to make better gameplay decisions. Developer Naughty Dog takes a very cinematic approach with the *Uncharted* series by putting the audience in the game by using filmic camera angles and jump cuts during the gameplay and cut scenes. More than any other series, the *Uncharted* franchise delivers on the decades-old game marketing cliché, "It's like playing a movie."

In a shooter game, it's important to know what the player is shooting at, and—perhaps more importantly—why. The game narrative supplies, or helps to justify, rich variations of enemy types, weapon types, and player goals. Even a game whose story would seem to have a very thin plot (*Left 4 Dead*) plunges the player into a rich environment populated by hordes of monstrous zombies—and only three other characters to ally with.

Perhaps no other genre is more dependent on story than the role-playing game (RPG). This genre is descended both from table-top RPGs like *Dungeons & Dragons* and from text-parsing computer games such as *Adventure* and *Hunt the Wumpus.*

---

18 Juul, loc. 1815

In both single-player RPG series (*Elder Scrolls, Fallout*) and massively multiplayer online games (*World of Warcraft, EVE Online*), the world is enormous. Players get caught up in both the lore of the world and the backstory of its characters. It provides a context for the epic adventure the players embark upon as they grow their characters.

But Story Is Less Important . . .

Tetris is one of the most popular games ever, yet it lacks a story. Puzzle games rarely need them. Why string the pretty gems together in *Bejeweled*? It doesn't really matter; it's just fun.

In sports simulations such as the *Madden* or *NBA Live* series, it may not matter much to many players. While professional sports does a great job of promoting a narrative with lots of history and tradition, the appeal of a sports video game is that it allows the players to pretend that they are playing as their favorite star athletes. Players can throw a touchdown, kick a goal, win a boxing match. Season-long strings of games or "franchise" modes can permit a player to fantasize about their favorite team (say, the Chicago Cubs or the Cleveland Browns) winning the World Series or the Super Bowl (now *those* would be fantasy games). But such stories—fantastic as they are—are private to the individual player.

However, there is an amazing amount of writing that goes into these "stories." Each game within the game has its own narrative, its own beginning, middle, and end. The announcers of the game (voiced by professional sports commentators) narrate the events of the game as it unfolds. It is scripted so that the announcers react to the scenario unfolding. If a quarterback is injured or is having a bad game, the player of the game hears the commentary as if it were a real NFL game. The *Madden* writers work all year long to give the *Madden* announcers meaningful things to say that change depending on the game situation and a particular onscreen athlete's record, both in the current digital game and In Real Life (IRL).

In racing games like the *Gran Turismo* or *Burnout* series, the driver is assumed to be the player and is almost never seen. In strategy games such as *Rise of Nations* and the *Civilization* series, the world is important for the context of the gameplay, but the player knows very little about her "commander" character. And yet, even these genres tout their stories—even if it's just a "career mode"—as key selling points. The game makers do their best to create an emotional arc in the gameplay so that games do not seem random. The player feels like he or she is moving toward a goal. Without goal, there is no story—even in the *FIFA* games, where the goal is to score a GOALLLLLLL!

But Exceptions Abound

Of course, there are many exceptions. World War II shooter games like *Call of Duty* tend to have neither memorable characters nor suspense, as the player knows that the Allies will eventually win and the Axis powers are destined to lose. Ditto most games set in the American Civil War. (However, with the move from World War II to the near-future settings of its *Modern Warfare* titles, the *Call of Duty* franchise has earned a reputation for delivering a new, action-movie-style story mode each year featuring name-brand Hollywood talent like screenwriter David Goyer and actor Kevin Spacey.)

There are story-driven puzzle games. One of the more popular and story-rich of these is *Portal*, in which the player character Chell is challenged by an artificial intelligence named GLaDOS (Genetic Lifeform and Disk Operating System) to complete each escape puzzle in the Aperture Science Enrichment Center using the portal gun. GLaDOS promises to serve cake when Chell clears all the levels. Cake is a great goal. So is staying alive.

The *StarCraft* and *Command & Conquer* series are real-time strategy games with deep stories and vivid characters. *StarCraft* is developed by Blizzard Entertainment, the company behind the *Diablo* series and *World of Warcraft*. Blizzard creates very rich worlds for its players to explore and vivid, complex characters for its players to identify with (or fight against). The company's focus on narrative—side by side with polished gameplay—is one of the main reasons for its worldwide success.

But not every player pays the same amount of attention to the story you've slaved over for months. If you can't handle that, you're in the wrong medium. In spite of the fact that *Call of Duty*'s story mode costs millions of dollars, some players skip it. Players skip cut scenes. Players play without listening to a game's dialogue, sound effects, and music score, sometimes preferring to plug in their own playlists. It happens. Get over it.

Blizzard's *World of Warcraft* team spends a vast amount of time, energy, and money on crafting the "lore" of the world of Azeroth. The quest writers are very careful to set the requirements of each individual mission—of the probably tens of thousands available in the game—in the context of the *world*. Indeed, every single quest is written as a little story. And yet, thousands of players each day click past these little stories, never reading them. So why does Blizzard bother? Why do so many successful game developers spend so much time on the craft of game narrative? Because they know that—whether consciously or unconsciously—players will develop a deep emotional connection to the game world that will keep them coming back again and again.

IMMERSION: CONTEXT IS EVERYTHING

Good story-driven games create worlds that players want to escape into, even for a brief play session on their coffee break or between train stops. Ballistic physics games have been around for decades, but it took the context of egg-stealing green pigs and vengeful fowl to turn that mechanic into the billion-dollar industry that is *Angry Birds*. In the strictest sense, gameplay doesn't *need* story, but story, context, justification, lore, metaphor, setting, and mood all help to bring the gameplay closer to the player, and the player closer to the gameplay.

Our focus as game writers should constantly be how best to merge story and gameplay so that a player's emotions and actions become one. So that the players are not just rewarded for killing the dragons and saving the princess, but feel emotionally fulfilled; as if they have not just watched a great adventure, but they have lived it. This feeling of participation—*immersion* into the game—is what games can do so much better than movies and television and novels. In announcing his development deal with Valve, *Star Wars* director J. J. Abrams observed that because gamers steer the action rather than passively viewing it, "in many cases, games are better at telling stories than movies."[19]

Games place the players in the world, enable them to make choices that influence the outcome of the narrative, and then experience the consequences of those choices. They get to be the hero.

STORY ≠ PLOT

Would you watch a movie with the following premise?

> You are a nameless pilot commanding a small spacecraft in a hostile asteroid belt. At your disposal you have an endless supply of laser blasts and a hyperspace button that transports your ship at random—either out of harm's way or right into the path of an asteroid. Oh, and a series of rogue flying saucers appear frequently which seem intent on blowing you to tiny pieces.

This was the scenario of the hit space shooter that burst through arcades in the late 1970s: *Asteroids.* No matter how many quarters players fed these hungry arcade machines, they never found out *who* was in the space ship, *why* they were in the middle of an asteroid field, or *what* were those evil flying saucers that became smaller and faster and harder to destroy. Yet despite leaving so many open questions—movie critics might call them "plot holes"—*Asteroids* was a genre-defining success.

But is there a *story* in *Asteroids*? Our quest now is to define "story" against the dynamic landscape of interactive narrative. What elements comprise a story? Do these elements appear in video games? Can we compare the stories of movies like *Star Wars* and *Marvel's The Avengers* to those of such games as *Far Cry, StarCraft, Braid,* or even *Asteroids*?

A STORY TUTORIAL

From the beginning of language, the act of telling stories has served to teach, bond, excite, and calm. Perhaps the first stories were told as

---

19 http://variety.com/2013/digital/news/j-j-abrams-will-develop-half-life-portal-games-into-films-1118065765/

factual accounts of that day's hunting or gathering expedition. Then humans—being human, after all—soon learned that embellishing on these stories had the effect of holding their listeners' attention. Percival H. Caveman soon realized his story was better if he survived an attack from a *saber-toothed-tiger* rather than a mere wild boar. (Better yet, *two* saber-toothed tigers!) Storytellers would remember their most popular tales and repeat them on request. They began to invent mythical stories of heroes, kings, gods, and monsters in order to make sense of—to *contextualize*—such mysteries as thunder, or storms, or death.

Just as stories are composed of sentences whose structure can be expressed as

Subject + Verb + Object = Sentence

the basic structure of stories themselves could be expressed as

Protagonist + Goal + Conflict + Obstacles + [Resolution] = Story

("Resolution" is in brackets, as sometimes game stories suspend resolution indefinitely, or have variable outcomes.)

From the standpoint of structure, there is little difference between the biblical story of Noah and *BioShock*. No, Noah didn't have to upgrade himself and become a Big Daddy—but both works share a common goal: to get out of the middle of the ocean and back to dry land.

Protagonist

In classic storytelling the protagonist is the hero of the story; he or she is the character who embarks on the adventure. Luke Skywalker is the hero of *Star Wars Episode IV: A New Hope*. It follows his journey off the desert world of Tatooine and into the world of the Rebel Alliance. His father, Anakin (Darth Vader), is the hero of *Star Wars III: Revenge of the Sith*. It follows his journey off Tatooine and into the world of the Galactic Empire.

In video games, the protagonist of *Beyond Good and Evil* is Jade; in *Mass Effect* the protagonist is Commander Shepherd; in *BioShock*, Jack.

In a Mario Bros. game, it is Mario. The protagonist is the one whose story we follow. The heroes hold our attention as we help them try to achieve their goal. And in video games and interactive narrative, it is usually the persona we are playing as. The protagonist is the player and vice versa.

Novels, movies, and especially television programs often have multiple protagonists. No single one of the friends on *Friends* was the protagonist of that series. Each was the protagonist of their own story line, depending upon the particular needs of the episode or the season-long arc. One-player games generally only have one protagonist—the player character—as it would be difficult, if not confusing, for a player to keep track of multiple individual personas as they played the game (though some games have tried this). In a two-player cooperatively played game like *Lego Star Wars* and its progeny, neither player is the protagonist; the team is the protagonist. But each player is the hero of her or his own experience playing through the story toward the . . .

Goal

All stories are about desire. Even if the desire is merely to survive or to be left alone. If no one wants anything, or is pursuing anything, then a story's not interesting. One of the oldest sayings in journalism is: "When dog bites man, that's not news. If man bites dog, that's news!" But what if man bites dog then dog plots revenge? Now that's a story! We'd totally see that movie or play that game.

We humans are driven by our desires, both base (food, water, air) and lofty (self-esteem, respect, creative expression). We relate to stories—fictional or not—about people trying to achieve things because we spend our days in similar struggles, if on smaller scales. Some protagonists want to change their lives for the better; others want their lives to return to a peaceful status quo after a crisis. But they all want something. And it's usually something obtainable. In the movie *National Treasure*, everyone is looking for actual treasure. That is the goal.

What the hero wants is the key to the story. Frank Daniel, the legendary screenwriting teacher, suggested that the plot of all movies is a variation on "somebody wants something and is having trouble getting it."[20] Back to the Bible and *BioShock*: Noah wants to save all the animal species of Earth and to survive the flood with his family. Jack wants to escape from Rapture, the underwater utopian world.

Without a clear goal, there is no direction, either for the protagonist or the player. In *Star Wars Episode IV: A New Hope*, Luke wants to rescue the princess and stop the Death Star. The goal is never achieved easily, nor should it be. Easily achieved goals make for dull stories.

Exciting stories, like exciting sporting matches, pit two combatants against each other in a situation where only one can win. For every protagonist there ought to be an antagonist.

Conflict

Conflict is what slows the protagonist down. Conflict is an axle-shattering pothole on the road to achievement. Without conflict there is no interest, and hence no story. A hundred years ago, Scottish critic William Archer observed that "human nature loves a fight, whether it be with clubs or with swords, with tongues or with brains."[21]

Remember those asteroids—that's conflict. If one of them hits you— you're dead.

Conflict can come from the environment, from other characters in the story, or it can be internal conflict such as guilt or self-doubt. The purest and most personified conflict is with the antagonist, who is sometimes the villain of the story, but sometimes is not. In the *Footloose* movies, the dance-hating pastor isn't a villain per se—he's a concerned father and a man of the cloth. He bans dancing for what he believes are good reasons. And yet, he's the story's antagonist. Either dancing will be legalized, or it will remain illegal. Our hero wants the former; the pastor wants the latter. They can't both achieve their opposing goals.

Sometimes the antagonist is a force of nature, as in *A Perfect Storm*,

---

20 Gulino, Paul. *Screenwriting: The Sequence Approach*. New York: The Continuum International Publishing Group Inc, 2006.

21 Archer, William. *Playmaking: A Manual of Craftsmanship*. Boston: Small, Maynard and Company, 1912.

or God. In the Book of Genesis, Noah is chosen by God to escape the liquid wrath that He will bring down to wash the wicked from the world.

In most cases, the antagonist of the story is also a villain, nogoodnik, a malefactor, evil, or a jerk. In the opening moments of *BioShock*, we see that Andrew Ryan, the antagonist of the story, is a classic "evil genius" type of villain. The player character, Jack, wants to escape the underwater city and return to civilization. Ryan, who believes Jack is a spy sent from the governments of the surface world, vows to kill Jack so that he can never return to the surface. Again, only one man can prevail. And since we are playing as Jack—we are rooting for him. At the time of this writing, *Evolve* debuted in demo mode. It's a game that pits hunters vs. alien monsters. Protagonists and antagonists. It's a multi-player game where one of the players plays as the monster.

A quick word about villains: they think they're *actually the good guys* in the story. Andrew Ryan really wanted to build a utopian paradise under the sea. It was everyone else who screwed that up.

Obstacles

Like the player of a game, the hero of a story must overcome challenges and obstacles. Unlike the player, the hero isn't doing it for mere entertainment. Players love obstacles; heroes don't.

And yet, for a story to hold our interest, the hero must be plagued by obstacles. Best laid plans must go awry. Normal situations must get all fouled up.

A protagonist in a TV show, novel, or film might react to obstacles with despair, the way Indiana Jones reacted to snakes in *Raiders of the Lost Ark*: "Why'd it have to be snakes?" The player-protagonist of a video game might say: "Cool! I get to fight snakes!"

In both versions of the movie *Ocean's Eleven* (filmed with Frank Sinatra in 1960 and rebooted in 2001), the teams hatch elaborate plots to steal money from multiple casinos. The plot of both films follows Danny Ocean's men as they carry out their plans and overcome roadblocks and setbacks that might have sent them all to jail. In the 2001 version starring George Clooney, Brad Pitt, et al., some of the obstacles include: Livingston leaving his portable monitor in the server room, Livingston getting lost, Saul's performance anxiety, Rusty's beef with Danny for not telling him about Tess, the city workmen fixing the weakness Basher was going to exploit to cut the power on fight night, Chen injuring his hand during the pinch heist, Benedict's men locking Danny in a storage room, the dead batteries in the detonator, and, of course, Bucky Buchanan from Saratoga.

Can we beg one more movie reference? Writers are like repo men. They are often introverted, sensitive, empathetic, and diplomatic. But on the page, they have to be agents of chaos and disorder. One of our favorite quotes is from the Alex Cox movie *Repo Man*: "An ordinary person spends his life avoiding tense situations. A repo man spends his life getting into tense situations." So do good writers.

These tense situations cause dramatic tension as the audience roots for the heroes to succeed. In each case, the audience sees how the obstacle could derail the plan, they fear for the heroes, then they delight as the heroes overcome the obstacle. In video games, the player is the one who overcomes the obstacles. These obstacles, enemies, and puzzles make up the gameplay content.

Resolution

Good stories need satisfying endings. The curiosity and emotional investment the audience has placed in the protagonist's quest must be resolved somehow. Even in linear narrative, the viewer or reader has invested a certain amount of their lifespan following the story. They expect closure.

The ending need not be happy, but it should be satisfying. The end of *Titanic* doesn't show Rose and Jack frolicking in New York City. Instead, Jack freezes to death. It is reasonably satisfying, however, and it certainly resolves the story. Jack sacrifices himself so that Rose can survive. The end of *Inception* is open-ended. Is the world real or not real? Did you find it satisfying?

In similar manner, all video game stories tend to resolve, even if what ends the story is the death of the player character and a "game over" message.

So back to our simple formula:

Protagonist + Goal + Conflict + Obstacles + [Resolution] = Story

Using that structure: Does the game *Asteroids* have a story? Of course it does:

Player Ship + Survival + Rogue Saucers + Asteroids + [Inevitable Player Death] = *Asteroids*

Plot & Story

The concept of story should be applied very broadly when discussing video games and interactive narrative. It's not just the plot. There may be no plot. In a video game, story is synonymous with the world of the game. One could argue that there is no real "plot" to *World of Warcraft* other than player progression. And yet one of the reasons that *WoW* is so successful is that Blizzard has created such a very deep and rich world for players to explore.

Most of the story of the player character in *WoW* is told through the quests, especially the class-specific or race-specific (e.g., paladin-only or human-only) quests. But that doesn't mean that *WoW* lacks a "real" story. The term *backstory* refers to events that happened to a character before the story began, and is often revealed through flashbacks or prologues. Bruce Wayne's backstory tells us that as a child he saw his parents murdered in cold blood by a petty thief, and this emotional trauma led him as an adult to create his Batman persona. In video games, the term "lore" refers to the backstory of the game world. The worlds of *Fallout, Mass Effect, Halo, Fable,* etc., are all rich in lore. It is in the midst of that lore that we as players engage in our own private stories through our avatars. In *The Elder Scrolls V: Skyrim*, you can complete the main quest/story line of the game and play to completion in about seven hours. (You can also jog through the Louvre in a few minutes. But why would you?) The world of *Skyrim* is so rich that players craft their own adventures, finding their own "stories," setting their own goals within that world.

Storytelling in games is more often a task of world building rather that plot writing.

A CRIMINALLY BRIEF HISTORY OF GAME NARRATIVE

Even though (analog) games have been around since the dawn of civilization, we're focusing here not on games themselves but on "story" (remember our broad definition) in games.

Chess

The *ur*-game in terms of narrative would be chess: the clash of two kingdoms for domination that was exciting because it had conflict. Chess also had characters: the bishop, the pawn, the knight, the queen, and the king. It had intriguing characters. Who's the most powerful person in the kingdom? It's not the king—he's kind of a figurehead. It's the queen, who can move wherever she wants. Each "character" has different abilities. The playing cards that became popular centuries later in the medieval period took their inspiration from the chessboard: kings, queens, knaves (jacks) and groups of faceless pawns.

Prussian War Games

In the early nineteenth century some Prussian officers developed a system that combined strategy, tactics, terrain, troop strength, and many other real-world conditions, and then simulated the chaos of warfare using . . . dice. They called this *Kriegsspiel* (war play), and it allowed them to train commanders and to simulate possible combat scenarios without having to pay for all the ammunition and property damage, not to mention wear and tear on the troops themselves. They were able to develop very specific new methods for attacking a specific town or defending a specific bridge against a specific opponent.

This system was used by Prussia's version of the Pentagon, and it was credited for enabling Prussia to crush France during the Franco-Prussian War.[22]

But one of the unintended effects of *Kriegsspiel* is that the Prussians realized that it was *a lot of fun*. (Yes, we wrote "Prussians" and "fun" in the same sentence.) They began to play it after hours and at home in the barracks and elsewhere. So it took not too long for *Kriegsspiel* to become commercialized and sold to the public

---

22 Murphy, Brian. *Sorcerers & Soldiers: Computer Wargames, Fantasies and Adventures* (Morris Plains, New Jersey, Creative Computing Press) 1984, p. 7.

as an entertainment. Even H. G. Wells (remember him from *The War of the Worlds*?) developed and published a rule book for hobbyist *Kriegsspiel*, published as *Little Wars* in 1913.[23]

Industrial Revolution = Leisure Time

While the Prussians were rolling dice in their forts, the Industrial Revolution was in full force through much of Europe and some of North America. An unintended consequence of so many men (and some women, and many kids) moving from the field to the factory was that suddenly the concept of leisure—time you didn't have to spend working—was destigmatized and became less sinful. The working class found themselves with time on their hands—just like the aristocrats—and very often filled that time as the gentry had always done: playing games. Board games and playing cards were mass marketed and became very popular.

Being mass marketed, though, many board games played very much alike. A vast number were dice races: roll the dice, race around the board. But what made each product unique was the story—the game world. Narrative was used to differentiate the products.

Board games remained very popular throughout the twentieth century. They brought the whole family together across the dinner or coffee table. In the '60s and '70s there was an explosion of board games designed to be sold on TV—among them *Operation*, *Battleship*, and *Hungry, Hungry Hippos*—which remain very popular today.

The Dawn of the Video Game

The generally agreed-upon birth date of the video game is 1961, with the development of *Spacewar!* at the Massachusetts Institute of Technology (MIT). It was developed on a huge (to us) "minicomputer," and the only people who could play it were students on campuses with computer departments or computer operators at businesses with computers. Or military guys with computers. If you weren't at a school or a research lab or a military installation or an insurance company, you didn't even know that video games existed.

But transistors and electronic miniaturization brought the size and cost of computing down, until by the late '60s you could put a tiny (for the time) single-purpose computer in a small (for the time) box. This allowed Ralph Baer to develop what became the Odyssey System for the living room and Nolan Bushnell to develop *Pong* for bars and pinball arcades. Bushnell parlayed his success with *Pong* machines into a home version, and that very quickly gave rise to the Atari 2600. Mattel countered

---

23 http://www.bbc.com/news/magazine-22777029

soon thereafter with the Intellivision system, and video games became a permanent fixture in many households.

Was there story to many of these games? No, not much at all. Were there characters? No. The only narrative was the premise, which was just paper thin, just barely enough to hang gameplay on.

Dungeons & Dragons

In the meantime, if you wanted a really rich narrative experience you played something like *Dungeons & Dragons*, which is a direct descendent of *Kreigsspiel*. Rather than moving an army or a squad around, however, in *D&D* you played as one individual character, and you developed a *very* close relationship with them. You role-play as that character, speaking with a distinct voice, interacting with other players, who are in turn speaking in their characters' voices. *D&D* has been described as being similar to an improvised radio play. Players react to the story being told by the dungeon master with both dialogue and dice rolling. The object of playing *D&D* is not to win, because your relationship with your character never ends. Your character keeps evolving, growing, and becoming more skillful as they (and you) experience each new scenario.

The reason it continues to be popular today is the imaginative play that it and its imitators and play-alikes create for the player. The getting involved in a tense situation and deciding how your character would react to that situation. *D&D* exploded, capturing the imagination of adults, college students, and teenagers, because it was so rich in narrative, and the world—Tolkienesque medieval fantasy—seemed at the time fresh and new.

The Computer Goes Home

Remember those college kids and lonely computer operators at the insurance companies? Throughout the '70s, they wrote and traded games to play on their closet-sized mainframe systems. As powerful as they were (at the time), the majority of these computers only supported text displays. They couldn't draw graphics onscreen, even simple *Spacewar!*-style vector graphics. "Text adventure" games like *Adventure* and *Hunt the Wumpus* became very popular because they were playable on most institutional computers and because, having only text to work with, the good ones brought players into (then) fresh and exciting worlds where they could enter dungeons and slay dragons. (Sound familiar?)

With the rise of personal computers in the very early 1980s, the text-parsing games like *Adventure* and table-top role-playing games like *D&D* merged into a single-player RPG experience. The earliest of these games were essentially text adventures with some limited onscreen graphics, but they soon evolved to "graphical adventure" games like *King's Quest*.

Myst: The World Is the Story, the Story Is the World

Myst was a graphical adventure game that used the technology of the multi-media PC—with all its sound cards and its (then) high-resolution color displays and the (then) vast amounts of data that could be stored on a CD-ROM—to create a truly immersive experience that captivated a huge audience and elevated the status of video games as something an adult could play without embarrassment.

In *Myst* both story and world were foregrounded. The player is transported to a fantastic world that Atrus, himself a writer, created through magic books. You pass through several "ages" of the world, exploring and solving complex puzzles, trying to discover the secret of the island and the family drama you've been sucked into. It was one of the very first games that got players and critics thinking that games could be something that might approach art.

―――

For us, story always wins. It builds the game world and creates a more immersive experience for the player. We think there is room for all types of stories to be played out on these new platforms—from the latest home consoles to the humble Internet browser.

It should all begin with story. But what about gameplay? How do you resolve the two as they compete for the player's attention?

Stay tuned.

Exploring the Game World

1 EXPLORE THE WORLD OF VIDEO GAMES

Writers write. And gamers play. We agree with the theory that Malcolm Gladwell laid out in his book *Outliers*—if you put 10,000 hours into something, you are going to get really good at it. So we want you to play 10,000 hours of video games.

Really?

Well, yes. If you want to transform your passion into profession, you have to know the world better than anyone else.

But you need to know both video games and the video game *industry*. Much more often than in Hollywood, game production methods are constantly being disrupted by new technology, new types of gameplay, news ways of making money (or not). It is crucial for any would-be game creator to be reasonably up-to-date as to the state of the games industry.

So this ongoing assignment is to find a game news outlet and follow it regularly. Record new ideas or reflections in your Game Journal.

FOLLOW TWO GAME SITES A DAY

Here are a few of our favorites. Try to focus on sites that feature industry news, not just consumer-focused game previews and reviews.

Bluesnews.com	This venerable site is a daily aggregation of the latest in game news.

Gamasutra.com	"The Art and Business of Making Games"—This site is closely affiliated with the Game Developers Conference and is filled with an overwhelming amount of news, blogs, and how-to's.
GamesIndustry.biz	The closest thing in the games business to *Daily Variety* or *The Hollywood Reporter*.
Gametrailers.com	Spend some time getting to know hot new and upcoming games.
KillScreenDaily.com	Dedicated to exploring games as art and culture.
Kotaku.com	A daily blog that focuses on what is happening in the world of games and game culture.
PocketGamer.co.uk	News and reviews of the latest in mobile and hand-held games.
Polygon.com	A superb source of news and in-depth feature articles.
RetroGamer.net	Don't feel like dusting off that old game console? A look at RetroGamer.net, devoted to games of the past, will change your mind.

LISTEN TO TWO PODCASTS A WEEK

There are many podcasts out there that claim to cover the gaming world. Many of these are in need of editing. But here are three we think you should begin to download.

Major Nelson Radio (majornelson.com/podcast) features Xbox Live's Larry Hryb and his co-hosts interviewing game developers and cultural influencers. This show is so popular it fills auditoriums at many video game conventions.

Idle Thumbs (www.idlethumbs.net) is produced by game developers, journalists, and fans who share the experience and enthusiasm of video games, both mainstream and independent.

"Gaming discussion from a different perspective" is the premise of Isometric (isometricshow.com), hosted by Brianna Wu, Maddy Myers, Steve Lubitz, and Georgia Dow.

LOCK YOURSELF IN THE GDC VAULT

The Game Developers Conference is the largest professional video game convention in North America. The GDC Vault (www.gdcvault.com) contains a wealth of information in the form of videos and slide presentations from thousands of industry leaders on a wide variety of video game development topics. (Hundreds of their presentations are available for free.). Choose a topic and start learning.

2 IMAGINE YOUR GAME WORLD

Throughout the rest of the exercises in this book, we'll be working toward helping you create a Game Concept Document that will help to document your very own game idea. The notes you take in your Game Journal will serve as inspiration; your imagination will do the rest.

Write down ten ideas (two sentences each) you have for a new video game. Put this list away.

The next day, having slept on it, choose three of the ten ideas. Add one or two sentences to your descriptions if you like. Put this short list away again.

The third day, choose one of the three. This is now the idea for what we will refer to as Your Game. Congratulations! Spend some more time thinking about Your Game and record any new notions in your Game Journal.

CHAPTER 03

ARISTOTLE VS. MARIO

THE CHALLENGE OF GAME WRITING

In a writers' room of a TV show, that moment when a great idea is pitched—and everyone in the room knows it's a great idea—is called the "peanut butter and chocolate" moment. Why peanut butter and chocolate? Some argue that peanut butter and chocolate is the greatest pairing ever that results in something even better. The sum is greater than the component parts, to mangle the old saying. Peanut butter + chocolate = awesome!

Storytelling and video games should be peanut butter and chocolate. They should go together smoothly and creamily. The content and the delivery system should perfectly sync. The medium allows for great production values filled with epic music, stunning graphics, and the same motion capture acting that turns Andy Serkis into Gollum and Cesar. But it's not that easy. Haris Orkin, writer of *Dead Island: Riptide,* has said that games "are the most complicated medium to write for, partly because we're still figuring out how to do it."[24]

Why is that? One might argue that the technology of Xbox and PlayStation has now caught up to the storytellers. Let's face it: Some of the earlier renderings of game worlds do not help much with the suspension of disbelief. But it's not all about visuals. Here's a quote from a *New York Times* review of a big blockbuster movie that talks about the new age of special effects: "Startling visual effects are fairly commonplace by now, yet there's always room for more . . ."[25]

---

24 http://kotaku.com/5988751/what-in-the-world-do-video-game-writers-do-the-minds-behind-some-of-last-years-biggest-games-explain

25 http://www.nytimes.com/movie/review?res=9404E3DD123DEE3ABC4851DF-B166838A679EDE

Guardians of the Galaxy? Gravity? Avatar? The visual effects in those movies are so good that their fantastic worlds seem hyperreal. But, no. The quote above is from 1961, about a movie called *Voyage to the Bottom of the Sea*. (It's a fun movie, by the way. See it!)

Story is where the problems begin between video games and the "passive" (noninteractive) media. Why? We think it is because:

> There is an inherent conflict between storyteller and audience when you give the audience some control over the narrative.

Video games are unlike any other medium. The movies and television are closer cousins to plays (the original form of dramatic storytelling) than video games. Who, ultimately, is the author of the experience? The writer or the player?

We like to express this conflict as . . .

ARISTOTLE VS. MARIO: THE CLASH OF STORY AND GAMEPLAY

Aristotle was a Greek philosopher and scientist who in 335 B.C. wrote the *Poetics*, a treatise on dramatic theory that is still studied—because it's still valid—today.

Mario is a pudgy Italian plumber from the Mushroom Kingdom who spends much of his time looking for Princess Peach. He is the creation of Shigeru Miyamato, who burst on the scene with *Donkey Kong* in 1981.

For someone who was watching a lot of Greek tragedies performed on a stage and written on papyrus with no CGI effects, Aristotle got a heck of a lot of it right. He is credited with the idea that *plot is character revealed by action*. The traditional principles of story structure as handed down from Aristotle have evolved from theater to novels to film and television, and to video games.

We look at Aristotle as the story guy and at Mario as the game guy. By highlighting the differences between the two, we can see the obstacles that video game creators have thrown in their path every day and can examine how successful gameplay designers, creative directors, and narrative designers are getting it right.

Aristotle: The Author-Defined Story

The main force of dramatic narrative is the author of the play. (We say play here, but please think of traditional "passive" media such as film and television. The author creates the characters and moves them through the plot. The author tells a story and evokes emotion in the audience that sits, passively, and does not participate in the story. That author-defined story creates "tragic pleasure, or catharsis experienced by fear and pity"[26] in the spectators.

Mario: The Player-Defined Story

In video games, the protagonist and player are one and the same. The player controls the actions of the protagonist. Yes, the author (the gameplay and narrative designers) funnels the player through the narrative with missions and quests and goals, but the player ultimately has control. In more open world games, the non-linear, free-roaming nature of the game gives players even more power to create and control their own experience—their own story.

Aristotle: 3-Act Structure

Aristotle was a structuralist. He analyzed enough plays to determine that the most aesthetically successful ones had a clear structure to their stories. Although Shakespeare and others often wrote in five acts through the years, we've distilled that in the last century or so to a clear three-act structure (although American TV shows are written in four or five acts, depending upon how many commercial breaks there are).

Act One is the beginning, which introduces the characters and their problem(s), Act Two is the middle (although we like to call it the "muddle," since that's where things get complicated), and Act Three is the end, which resolves everything. Aristotle identified these phases of the story as the *protasis*, *epistaxis*, and *catastrophe*. (Or if you will—the beginning, middle and the end: setup, confrontation, resolution.)

---

26 *The Basic Works of Aristotle*. Ed. Richard McKeon Modern Library (2001) - Poetics. Trans. Ingrid Bywater, pp. 1453–1487.

In Hollywood, story structure suggests a chain of events that are easy for the audience to follow. A hero has a problem, a goal, and attempts to achieve that goal. The goal often involves a quest or a journey. It can be physical, like moving from the Shire to Mordor in *The Lord of the Rings* or emotional, like moving from mental illness to health in *A Beautiful Mind*. Every story structure book you ever read, or have heard of—from Lajos Egris's *The Art of Dramatic Writing* to Syd Field's *Screenplay* to Blake Snyder's *Save the Cat!*—has the same DNA as its ancient grandfather, Aristotle's *Poetics*.

Mario: Ad Hoc Structure

Mario represents video game structure, which we'll discuss more in the next chapter. If games have dozens, sometimes hundreds, of levels (or missions, or sub- and side quests), should we group these into three acts? The end of the first act, when the hero often embarks on her quest, comes about 30 minutes into a movie. That's *too late* for gamers. They want to start playing!

Maybe we could group most games into the following three "phases," if you will: Phase I is the Tutorial, in which the player learns the basics of how to play. Phase II would be the bulk of the game content—the levels. Phase III would be the ending, which should include the most challenging bits *and* some sort of cool end-game reward. Traditionally, this has been a final blast of narrative, but it's more rewarding when the players unlock some additional content or a new gameplay mode—something they can play as well as watch.

Aristotle: Finite Duration

A story ends. It arrives at its conclusion in a finite duration. We know a movie is roughly two hours. A television show might be an hour long. A television series might run from one to five years. A mini-series like *True Detective* follows the BBC formula and has a set number of episodes. Books have page numbers. E-books now helpfully tell you the percentage of the book you've read, and even estimate how many hours it will take you to finish based on how often you've been advancing the pages.

Even George R. R. Martin's *A Song of Ice and Fire* series of fantasy novels will someday, sadly, end.

Mario: Infinite Duration?

On the other hand, there is no set running time for a video game. They vary! When you start playing a game, it's very rare that you know how many levels you have in front of you. And that's just in linear games. In non-linear games, where players can pick their own path, so much of the experience, including the duration, is defined by the player. Craig Lafferty, the lead producer on *The Elder Scrolls: Skyrim* said that he esti-mates, "the main quests take you about 30 hours or so. And the additional content—we haven't played it all yet—but I'd guess two to three hundred hours of gameplay there. That's one thing we haven't scaled back on. We keep going bigger, crazier. More and more content and dungeons."[27] This seems great for us as players, but by his own estimate it would take you between 30 to 300 hours to "finish" *Skyrim*.

When will the online *Call of Duty* players "finish" *CoD*? When there are no more n00bs to conquer? When Activision shuts off the match-making servers?

Bob has been playing *WoW* for over 10 years (with a few breaks). It's why he doesn't have children, but he has a level 100 female gnome demonology warlock named Chocoba. (Keith, on the other hand, played fewer games but has watched way too many movies.) When will Bob be done with *WoW*? Blizzard will probably *have* to shut down its servers. And even then, he can continue to "play" in Azeroth thanks to the *WoW* board and trading card games, comic books, licensed novels, unlicensed fan fiction, etc.

Aristotle: The Audience Is Listening

The audience for passive media is always listening: watching the show or play. Reading the book. Most people stay for the length of a movie. Most people don't try to skip forward in a movie until they get to the parts

---

27   http://www.pcgamer.com/skyrims-main-quest-30-hours-long-additional-content-lasts-two-to-three-hundred-more/

they like. Although not everyone who starts a book may finish it, authors (and filmmakers, and dramatists) create their works under the assumption that *most* of their audience will be paying attention *most* of the time. Sadly, with games, it's different . . .

Mario: Wait, What?

Maybe the audience isn't listening. As important as we feel that story is to the overall experience of a game, we know that not all players play in the same way, or for the same reasons. Many players skip over the cinematics and get right into the action. You might say they are like people who text during a movie. We maintain that if the audience is vested in a story, they will not text during the movie, or skip the game cinematics. If they are involved with the outcome of the narrative, they are rewarded not just with gameplay rewards but a richer emotional experience.

One of the challenges in writing for video games is to change the way they are written. All writing is problem solving. Writers create characters and get them in and out of trouble. Video games are largely problem solving—for both creators and players. So let's look at one of the problems of writing for this relativity new medium. How is the game actually written? And what can the writer do?

MAKING THE DRAGON ROAR: ROLES IN A GAME STUDIO

Let's imagine you've been hired as a writer for a game studio. The blue sky period is over and the studio has decided the game is going to be about a *dragon*. Why? Who knows? The studio owner's kid wants a game about a dragon. The owner's husband had bad dreams about a dragon. Marketing says dragon games are selling like hotcakes. For now, all that's important is that the game centers around a dragon and you, the writer, have to come up with the greatest story ever for a game about a dragon because a year ago you had the good judgment to buy this book!

The questions start flowing: How many dragons? Can the dragon fly? Can it breathe fire? Where does it live? Does the player fight the dragon? Does the player ride the dragon? Is the player the dragon itself? What does the dragon look like? What does it sound like? Does it roar? Speak? Should it sound like Benedict Cumberbatch?

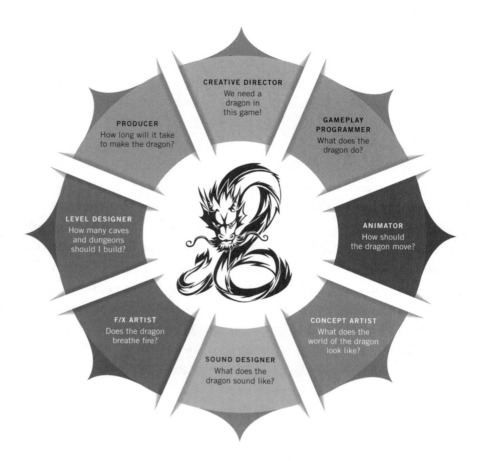

How will this dragon game be better than other dragon games?

All the creative teams are eager to get started. The concept artist wants to work with the environment artist to design the world. The level designers would want to know what the world contains, so that they can start thinking about obstacles and rewards. Can they set levels in caves, castles, shopping malls? What if dragons are born from volcanoes?

Does it have to be a dragon? Can't we make it a flatulent velociraptor?

All these questions come from the dozens of creative voices at the beginning of a game project. You need them all, and more, to make the dragon roar.

▬

HOW ARE GAMES WRITTEN? ARE THEY WRITTEN?

Playwrights came to Hollywood in the very early 1930s, at the dawn of the talkies. They did not adapt well. Movies are moving pictures. They are a visual experience. The adage in Hollywood script meetings is: show, don't tell. Playwrights did not know how to do that. They came to Tinseltown and wrote long speeches and wonderful pieces of dialogue. These were great for a play, but not for the visual medium of motion pictures. Meanwhile, those original screenwriters, who came up loving the "flicks," were getting pretty far along at learning to use a camera to tell a story. They were "writing the tech into their text." What we mean is: They recognized what film could do and began to craft their stories so that they played to the strengths of the medium. Soon great screenwriters like John Huston and Preston Sturges became directors. They were writers who knew that while the written word was very important, what was visual was vital.

We need storytellers who know tech and tech people who know storytelling. They cannot be exclusive. Susan O'Connor, who wrote for *BioShock, Far Cry 2,* and many other great games, said:

> The part that's most frustrating for me as a creative is that the industry tends to attract people who are really interested in technology, because you need a ton of programmers to make a game. You don't need a lot of writers to make a game, or animators, even. The percentage of the creatives in the game versus the percentage of technologists you need is totally out of whack. A lot of times, what ends up happening when you have a room of primarily tech-oriented [staff], it becomes like a software development environment.[28]

Just because in the past games have often been written by engineers does not mean things should stay that way. This is not to say there were not great creative directors and producers doing great work. Early games were programmed, they were not developed. It was all about what the tech could do. And that forced constraints on the storytelling. During our time working together on the game at the toy company as we tried to contextualize the gameplay with cool story elements in the

---

28 http://gameological.com/2013/05/susan-oconnor-game-writer/

for them. However, it also explains why all the nominees are from big publishers that can *afford* to sign the guild agreement.)

Another reason we believe we are in the golden age of interactive storytelling is how quickly the technology is evolving. Not just because of interactive fiction on tablets or games on all sorts of mobile devices, but also because of the expanding independent games scene. Just as cinephiles might go to a film festival or their local "art house" theater to find character-driven movies, TV viewers might forgo the big networks and choose premium cable or "streaming" networks for more nuanced storytelling, and video game creators in the thriving indie game scene are telling groundbreaking stories about things other than monsters and robots. Some of the best of these games are beginning to be recognized by the Independent Games Festival. These are the games that the IGF nominated for Best Narrative in 2014:

DEVICE 6—A surreal thriller in which the written word is your map, as well as your narrator. *DEVICE 6* plays with the conventions of games and literature, entwines story with geography, and blends puzzle and novella to draw players into an intriguing mystery of technology and neuroscience.

Dominique Pamplemousse in "It's All Over Once the Fat Lady Sings!"—Dominique Pamplemousse is an interactive musical comedy in stop motion, in which the titular protagonist is a down-on-their-luck private investigator of ambiguous gender only one rent payment away from homelessness.

Paralect—A 2D platformer that uses gameplay, visuals, and narrative to tell a personal story of cultural unrooting. It explores the paradigm shifts caused by culture shock and adaptation, and investigates how those transformations affect one's vision of people, their environment, the place you initially came from, and, most importantly, the place you wish to call home.

Papers, Please—The communist state of Arstotzka has just ended a 6-year war with neighboring Kolechia and reclaimed its rightful half of the border town, Grestin. Your job as immigration inspector is to control the flow of people entering the Arstotzkan side of Grestin from Kolechia.

The Yawhg—A one- to four-player choose-your-own-adventure game that randomizes a unique story every time you play. The evil Yawhg is returning. How will the town's locals lead their lives in the meanwhile, and what will they do when the dreaded Yawhg finally arrives?

The Stanley Parable—A first-person exploration game. You will play as Stanley, and you will not play as Stanley. You will follow a story, you will not follow a story. You will have a choice, you will have no choice. The game will end, the game will never end. Contradiction follows contradiction, the rules of how games should work are broken, then broken again. This world was not made for you to understand.[34]

HOW DO WE SOLVE THIS PROBLEM?

At the recent Future of Digital Media symposium at the S. I. Newhouse School at Syracuse University, Larry Hryb—better known as Xbox Live's "Major Nelson"—said that game stories are "3D storytelling." He is correct. No other medium has the potential to involve the audience as much as video game narrative. The legendary film critic Roger Ebert famously blogged that video games can never be art. We have mad respect for Roger and his legacy, but he obviously never played *Braid, Limbo, Journey, This War of Mine*, or any one of a growing list of independent games that are redefining the medium upward. Remember, it's now the golden age of television, but less than twenty years ago, TV was derided daily as "the Boob Tube." What changed?

---

34 http://www.igf.com/2014winners.html

Cable created new markets. Barriers to entry fell. There were more places for independent voices to be heard. HBO wanted to do something different from the traditional networks. Audiences tuned in.

What's changing now in video games is that we're just beginning to learn how we can get the gameplay and the stories to resonate with each other.

We feel we are seeing better games when there is a writer behind the wheel, or at least in the car when the drive to create the game begins.

Games are beginning to take a story-first approach. Story games such as *BioShock* are creator-driven. Ken Levine was the creative director of Irrational Games, the company that produced *BioShock*. He studied drama at Vassar.

He knows both drama and gameplay, and he and his team created an enduring masterpiece.

Neil Druckmann is the creative director/writer of *The Last of Us*. He majored in Entertainment Technologies at Carnegie Mellon. A convergence of story and tech.

BioWare is a company known for their story-driven games such as *Mass Effect*. Drew Karpyshyn—a novelist who majored in English—was the writer of many of those. David Jaffe, game director of the original *God of War*, went to the University of Southern California. Rather than attending its film school, he became a game designer, channeling his passion for storytelling into the interactive medium. Susan O'Connor studied English literature and art history. She brought her knowledge of story to the worlds of *BioShock* and *Far Cry 2*. Amy Henning (*Uncharted*) studied English literature at UC Berkeley before studying film at San Francisco State University.

We are not saying you have to get a degree in drama, or film, or English to create a great game—but you should learn to love story. Study it. Analyze it in other media. What do movies and television do well that games can co-opt? Remedy Entertainment, the creators of such work as *Max Payne, Alan Wake,* and *Quantum Break,* have a note for anyone who is looking to apply to work with their company. According to a recent job posting, they are looking for people with a "passion for story-driven games and movies, and the familiarity for the use of drama in those media."

Remedy describes its game *Quantum Break* in a way that perfectly sums up the potential of games as interactive narrative:

> *Quantum Break* blurs the line between television and gameplay, integrating the two into one seamless, uniquely immersive experience. It's a revolutionary entertainment experience that weaves the cinematic action of intense gameplay with the tension and drama of scripted television, creating a world where each has a direct impact on the other.[35]

Mario and Aristotle seem to be on a collision course. They're not. They are now on the journey together and as we move forward and examine game structure and gameplay and level design, we hope to show you what great story-driven games have shown us—that Mario and Aristotle need each other in order for the interactive medium to approach art.

---

35 http://remedygames.com/games/quantum-break

DRAGON EXERCISES 03

Expressing Your Game Idea

We now want to start focusing on video game narrative and how the combination of story and gameplay come together to create an immersive tale.

1 WATCH A "GAME MOVIE"

So many games, so little time. A game might take anywhere from a few minutes to a few dozen hours to complete. We want you to concentrate on the tale being told within the game. So fire up YouTube and watch a *game movie*, in which a fan has edited out the gameplay and stitched the cinematics together to form a (sometimes) coherent narrative experience. Search "game movie," pick one or two, and record your impressions—good and bad—in your Game Journal.

2 IMAGINE "JACK AND JILL: THE VIDEO GAME"

Create a video game narrative from the nursery rhyme "Jack and Jill":

> *Jack and Jill went up a hill to fetch a pail of water.*
> *Jack fell down and broke his crown, and Jill came tumbling after.*

Who is Jack? Who is Jill? Where do they live? What is the story genre? What is the game genre? How big is the hill? Is it guarded by a dragon? An army? Zombies? "Jack and Jill" may seem like a mundane story, but it doesn't have to be. Gameplay and obstacles will build the narrative into something exciting.

Write a one-paragraph description of your version of "Jack and Jill: The Video Game."

3 GAMEFLY EXERCISE

First of all, GameFly is an excellent service that rents games by mail. If you have a game console—hand-held or living room—GameFly is a great way to sample games before you commit to buying them, as well as to discover games you might have missed from their huge catalog.

Imagine you can see Your Game on the shelf at your favorite game retailer. What does it look like? What is the title? What is the tagline? What is on the cover? Using any images and fonts you can find on the Internet (and you can find a lot), create a mock-up video game box for Your Game. But don't stop there. Write the description that might appear on Your Game's listing on GameFly or on the back of its box. Browse GameFly.com and read the brief two- to three-sentence descriptions in the games' "Details" section for some examples.

continue their bromance by sitting down to play a board game. What game? Something new. Something they have never played before. They have to know the rules, and they have to know the structure. As players, what are they trying to accomplish? How will they do that? The game-play designer spent a lot of time thinking about how they funnel the players through the game, and about the story of the game. How well is that communicated to our players, Ari and M?

When they open the game board, they can see the structure of the game. There is a beginning, a middle, and an end. The players know they have to get from Point A to Point B. There are a number of obstacles along the way. It could be *Chutes and Ladders, Settlers of Catan,* or even *The Walking Dead* board game. You can look at the board and know where you have to go. Board games might be the only immersive experience where you see the structure of the game laid out in front of you. For most other media—film, television, comic books, interactive fiction, video games—the structure is hidden from the participant at the beginning. But that structure is always on the minds of the creators.

Frank Daniel was fond of telling the following anecdote to his Story Analysis class (which Bob was lucky enough to take, and has paraphrased here):

> A wandering student had traveled around the world in search of the secret of alchemy, the process of turning mere lead into shining gold. At last he found, atop a lonely mountain, a wizard who knew the secret and was willing to teach it. He showed the student the process, chanting an arcane spell over the Philosopher's Stone, and the student spent many days practicing before his new tutor until at last he was able to turn lead to gold at will. As he was leaving, the wizard said, "Oh, just one more thing. When you're doing this, never think about beavers. Otherwise, the process won't work." The student trudged home, sadder than sad, because he knew he would never *not* be able to think of beavers when trying to change lead to gold.

His point was that as a dramatic writer, once you know story structure, you will never *not* be able to see the structure of any movie you see, play you attend, book you read. It's a sacrifice you must be willing to make in order to understand the craft. The same is true of games. Once you study gameplay, you're always seeing the strings the designers use to make you dance like a puppet in their game world. The same is true of "spoiler alerts." Those are for amateurs, fanfolk, and the population at large. You should never avoid hearing how a story works (or doesn't) just because you haven't yet seen it. Expect spoilers. Don't run from them. Leave that to the civilians.

Writers, creative directors, and producers of video games do the same thing as screenwriters and TV show runners—they "board out" (storyboard) the structure of the movie or the series. The best game schools in the world all teach their fledgling gameplay designers to work out the game's structure and systems on paper—using board-game-style prototypes—before they set loose the programmers programming and the artists arting.

TRADITIONAL ENTERTAINMENT STRUCTURE = 3 ACTS

There have been many, many great books written about screenplay structure. At their most basic, they share the idea that movies are broken down into three acts:

Boy Meets Girl. Boy Loses Girl. Boy Gets Girl Back.

The cat goes up a tree. We fire laser beams at the cat. The cat comes down the tree in chunks. (Poor cat.)

Or as Aristotle's Greek peers would say: *protasis, epistaxis* (literally "nosebleed"), and *catastrophe*. Which basically means Act One (premise), Act Two (muddle, conflict), and Act Three (synthesis or resolution).

Or as our Aristotle's eye-rolling teenage kid would say: OMG! WTF? LOL!

ACT ONE	ACT TWO	ACT THREE
Setup	Confrontation	Resolution

Act One—The Setup

The first part of the structure is setting up the who, what, when, where of the story. Who is the protagonist? What is distinctive about them? Do we like them? Where is the story taking place? Toward the end of the act the writer will introduce the main problem for the hero. The First Act ends when we know what their plan is to set things aright. Will things go smoothly? Heck, no.

Act Two—Confrontation

As the heroes begin to execute their plan, they are confronted with obstacles, which are both numerous and annoying. (They have to be annoying, or it's not dramatic; just as puzzles have to be challenging, or they're not fun.) In his groundbreaking analysis *The Hero with a Thousand Faces*, Joseph Campbell distilled a number of stories and legends from the mythology of different cultures into a "monomyth" called "The Hero's Journey." Although this is *not the only story archetype*, it's one that works very well for video games. Once the hero embarks on his or her quest, they encounter a series of what Campbell calls Threshold Guardians. These are antagonists—other than the main villain—that the hero must defeat along the way. (In video games, you know them as Level Bosses.) They personify the many trials and sacrifices our hero(es) must overcome.

The Second Act is the middle and takes up the majority of the dramatic action: The confrontation. Things must fall apart. Centres cannot hold. The end of the Second Act is traditionally the *lowest point* in the story. The Dark before the Dawn. That dragon seems *freakin' invulnerable* and *refuses to be slain*. All seems lost.

Think of *Star Wars Episode IV: A New Hope*. Think of the lowest point in the story. The "all is lost" moment. When is it? It's got to be the *worst of all possible* situations. Is it when Our Heroes are sneaking through the most dangerous place in the galaxy, the planet-killing battleship known to its friends as the Death Star? Nope.

Is it when they're trapped in the jail on the planet-killing battleship? Nope.

Is it when they fall waist-deep in squalid muck inside the giant trash compactor below the jail on the planet-killing battleship? Nope.

Is it when they discover there's some type of amphibious tentacled monster under the surface of the squalid muck inside the giant trash compactor below the jail on the planet-killing battleship? Nope.

Is it when the walls start to close in, compacting the trash and Our Heroes inside the giant trash compactor below the jail on the planet-killing battleship? *Yes!*

Plus, just a few minutes later, Obi-Wan dies. It's a bummer. (We told you to expect spoilers.)

Act Three—Resolution

In Act Three, the protagonist(s) comes face to face with the antagonist and has to slay the dragon. Once slain, then the hero (and we) can at last return to normal—or to a new normal.

We can illustrate the three-act structure of linear narrative like this:

Many blockbuster story-driven games follow this formula. Developers grow up playing games, but they also watch movies. Many have emulated traditional Hollywood three-act structure to good success. Many are also adopting (and adapting) the traditional Hollywood process when it comes to creating the story for their games. "We use the traditional screenwriting process: a pitch, a synopsis, a scene outline, and a screenplay," said Sam Lake, creative director of Finland's Remedy Entertainment (*Max Payne, Alan Wake, Quantum Break*). "Lots of drafts of each and obviously lots of back and forth with gameplay and level design. Iteration and feedback loops are absolutely vital."[36] *God of War* game director David Jaffe has also likened the process of creating a game to writing a screenplay.[37]

ADD A MIDPOINT = 4 ACTS

But the thing is, most Hollywood movies work in *four* acts, not three. Screenwriters often talk about the midpoint of the movie, halfway through the second act—that's where a twist or a big reversal often comes. Allies turn into enemies; enemies to allies. Good movies are balanced. Act One is the same length as Act Three and Act Two is twice as long as either of them. For years, the rule of thumb was that a script for a typical two-hour movie should be 120 pages (one minute per page—that's why professional screenplays follow a very strict format). A balanced structure breaks down to 30 pages for Act One, 60 pages for Act Two, and 30 pages for Act Three.

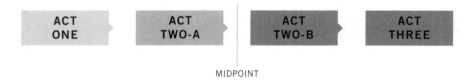

ACT ONE → ACT TWO-A → ACT TWO-B → ACT THREE

MIDPOINT

The midpoint is like a curtain at the intermission of a Broadway show—something big happens to the plot or the characters, hopefully both. This also occurs in *BioShock*: The midpoint is when Jack learns what has really been going on in Rapture and that he has been deceived and manipulated by the only friend (he thought) he had.

Are some movies now mimicking some video game structures, where the characters and the premise and the reactions to action drive the story to a midpoint exposition dump? For the answer, look no further than the movie *Wreck It Ralph*, which is set in the world of a video game. Halfway through the film, Ralph learns that, although it will break her

---

36 http://www.reddit.com/comments/1ewxtb/im_sam_lake_the_creatorwriter_of_max_payne_and

37 Crecente, Brian The man behind God of War is working on a new game ... and hunting ghosts? http://www.polygon.com/2013/9/20/4728152/the-man-behind-god-of-war-is-working-on-his-new-game-and-hunting

heart, Vanellope simply cannot compete in the big race. If she wins, her glitch will be revealed and the arcade manager will pull the plug on her game, "Sugar Rush." And in the big dramatic midpoint exposition dump, Ralph learns that everyone in the game might die. Of course, he was lied to by King Candy, but still, this twist keeps us going and makes us feel sad for both Ralph and Vanellope.

SHAKESPEARE AND THE HULK = 5 ACTS

If you remember your Shakespeare, his plays are divided into *five* acts. Media blogger Film Crit Hulk has argued passionately against three-act structure and believes we are now "back" to five-act storytelling.[38] (His structural comparison of *Romeo and Juliet* to *Iron Man* is great reading, ASSUMING YOU CAN GET PAST HIS ALL-CAPS STYLE, THAT IS.)

Many hour-long TV shows, be they police shows, courtroom or hospital dramas, or speculative fiction dramas like *Lost* or *Fringe*, are divided into five acts.

The five acts are:

ACT ONE—Introductions and Establishing a Pre-Existing Conflict

This idea lends itself well to video game narrative, where players don't have the patience for a lot of exposition and setting-up of conflict. The player wants to be dropped into the middle of the action—whether it be a *Call of Duty* or an indie game—so they can start to play. Setting your story in a conflict zone (like a war, or a high school campus), or around a main character at odds with himself is very economical. In *God of War*, we meet Kratos as he throws himself from a high cliff into the sea. He hates himself and wants to die.

Macbeth takes place in Scotland during a time of political turmoil, and Macbeth has just put down a rebellion against his king, Duncan. Macbeth is a competent general and loyal to Duncan, but he's restless and ambitious. (Pre-existing conflict, see?) He's told by three witches

---

38 http://badassdigest.com/2013/12/11/hulks-screenwriting-101-excerpt-the-myth-of-3-act-structure/

that he is fated to be king himself someday. After learning that Duncan will stay the night in their castle, Lord and Lady Macbeth decide to speed the process along.

ACT TWO—A Turn or Reversal Which Deeply Worsens the Main Conflict

This is where we learn what the "dragon" is and what the player needs to accomplish.

The Macbeths murder Duncan in his sleep and frame his bodyguards, whom Macbeth then kills in front of witnesses. Will he get away with it?

ACT THREE—A Major Turning Point. A Twist.
A Surprise that Makes Things Worse.

This is similar to the midpoint described in the last section. Assumptions have been overturned. Plans are destroyed and must be re-thought.

But Macbeth, now king, realizes that his hold on power is tenuous, and he feels as though he has to keep murdering those who threaten him, beginning with his dear friend Banquo and Banquo's son. He sends assassins to do this, but the son escapes. Macbeth, meanwhile, sees Banquo's ghost at dinner, and reacts with guilt and shame—in front of his court. Many of his lords question his sanity; some wish to join Duncan's son Malcolm in exile.

ACT FOUR—The Spiral

Things happen rapidly, one conflict driving to the next, toward the conclusion.

Macbeth, paranoid as ever, visits the three witches for further portents. They tell his fortune in ambiguous riddles, but Macbeth chooses to hear what he wants to hear: It will be a fight to keep his throne, but he is destined to prevail. He learns that a key ally, Macduff, has fled to join the resistance, so Macbeth has his family and servants slaughtered. Macduff, blinded by vengeful grief, joins Malcolm as they prepare to attack Macbeth's castle.

ACT FIVE—Climax/Resolution

Wherein things resolve. This is the part we have to sit through to get to the post-credits teaser for the next movie.

Lady Macbeth suffers from visions brought on by her guilt. Her mental and physical health decline rapidly, and she dies just before Malcom's army attacks. Macbeth, learning too late not to trust fortune tellers, is killed by a vengeful Macduff. Malcolm takes his place as the lawful king.

More acts, more acceleration of plot. More happening in the story. Of all the various media, video games can have the most narrative. (Remember that movies average two hours; many video games can easily last sixty to eighty hours.)

THE SEQUENCE APPROACH = 8 ACTS!

The sequence approach is another popular method of structuring your story. This takes the three acts and divides them into eight sequences, with each carrying a mini-objective that pushes toward the main objective.

Each sequence has its own dramatic context and its own beginning, middle, and end. The end of each sequence leads to the beginning of the next sequence. Each sequence has a mini-objective that needs to be accomplished before the protagonist can move on to the next.

This is sounding very much like levels in games, isn't it? Take an easy example: Compare the movie *Raiders of the Lost Ark* with the game *Lego Indiana Jones*. There's the great opening sequence where Indy has to escape the boulder. Then Indy has to fight the Nazis in the bar in Nepal. Later, Indy might be in the middle of a truck chase, or a fight in a bazaar. Each sequence is a new level that puts him on a new mission. It's the same in the movie, and in the game.

But there aren't just eight levels or missions in a game. There can be any number of missions or quests—the limits are essentially creation time, and the budget that flows from that schedule. Just as there can be any number of episodes in a TV series. What's important for both, however, is that one flows logically into the other. Because of level A, level B must happen.

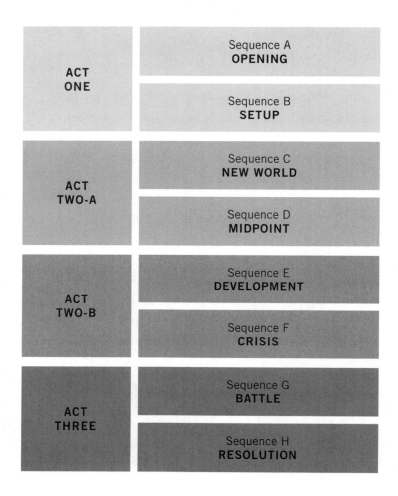

SERIALIZED STORYTELLING

One of the conventions in this new golden age of television (*The Sopranos,
Breaking Bad*) is serialized storytelling. There is a "what happens
next?" structure where the events of one week end in a cliffhanger or a
shocking revelation that keeps viewers tuning into the next week's episode. Remedy Entertainment's head of franchise development, Oskari
Hakkinen, has said that long-form TV stories—arcs that can last an
episode, a season, or a series—have influenced his studio's approach to
game narrative as much as movies have. When his team was developing
Alan Wake,

big series started to come out with HBO and what not, *Lost* for instance was one where people were buying the boxed sets, and then watching the episodes at their own pace. Some are bingeing through it, some are watching one a day, some are watching one every other day or once a week, but all at their own pace. [. . .] The great thing about it was each episode had its own three act structure and ended on a cliffhanger, which kind of prodded you on to see what happened next.[39]

As frequent binge watchers and game players ourselves, we can tell you that good episodes or game missions have a magic "potato chip" effect. Try eating just one potato chip: the first one makes you want the next one, and so on, and before you know it the bag's empty. The hero(es) has a goal and sets down the risk-laden path to achieve that goal. Along the way there are many adventures, each with its own beginning, middle, and end.

Telltales Games has had great success and acclaim from developing one of the first successful episodic video games. *The Walking Dead: The Game*—like AMC's *The Walking Dead* TV program—is based on *The Walking Dead* comic book series created by Robert Kirkman. Telltale has done the same with *The Wolf Among Us*, adapted from Bill Willingham and DC Comics' *Fables*. It is billed as "A Telltale Games Series," with each episode being a new game in the story.

Since the last "next" generation of game consoles (e.g., the Xbox 360 and PlayStation 3) came with robust Internet technology and big hard drives, downloadable content (DLC) has helped to keep many big AAA games alive with post-release spin-off and "sequel lite" adventures delivered in episodes. *Fallout 3, Borderlands, Grand Theft Auto IV, Dragon Age* and *Mass Effect* are among the many games that offer episodic downloadable game content to add another chapter to the story or to explore a different corner of the game world.

---

39 Chapple, Craig. "A Quantum Breakthrough: Remedy's quest for the perfect game narrative" http://www.develop-online.net/interview/a-quantum-breakthrough-remedy-s-quest-for-the-perfect-game-narrative/0187411, December 18, 2013.

BEGINNING, MIDDLE & ENDING(S)

We've discussed interesting structures that video games can adopt as their narrative framework, but what happens *within* those structures can be just as interesting. The interactivity that Mario represents has led to some very innovative storytelling possibilities. As with many advanced technologies, it's taken us a while as a culture to catch up with and understand all its implications.

Parallel Narrative

A video game might have a parallel narrative. If all protagonists (players) are after the same goal, then they are on the same path and the story can move forward with each of them.

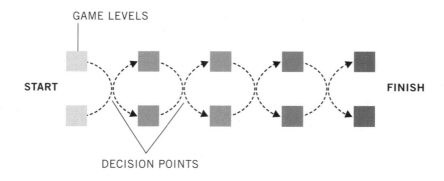

Throughout the game *Heavy Rain* players can play the same story events through the eyes (and bodies) of different characters, each time pushing the plot along. In *The Last of Us,* toward the end of the second act of the story, when the character of Joel is incapacitated, the player continues on as his companion, Ellie. *Grand Theft Auto V* allows you to switch at will between three different player characters (Michael, Trevor, and Franklin) over the course of the game. Playing as one PC, you might encounter one of your other avatars as an NPC (non-player character), just as Niko Bellic, protagonist of *GTA IV*, showed up as a guest star in that game's first DLC release, *The Lost and Damned.*

Branching Narrative

A branching narrative is a line of dramatic action that begins with the same problem but might end in any of a number of resolutions. Think of this as: beginning. middle. many endings. Its best known literary precursor is probably Bantam Books' "Chose Your Own Adventure" paperbacks from the late 1970s and '80s, and the form is now enjoying a comeback thanks to the arrival of e-books and touch-screen readers that make reading interactive fiction (IF) easier than ever before.

This formerly very niche medium is poised for its first blockbuster as more and more readers raised on video games are growing comfortable with the idea of becoming more of a participant in their narrative experiences. We will touch on interactive fiction occasionally throughout the book, but we believe that the fundamental principles of good game writing apply to good IF writing.

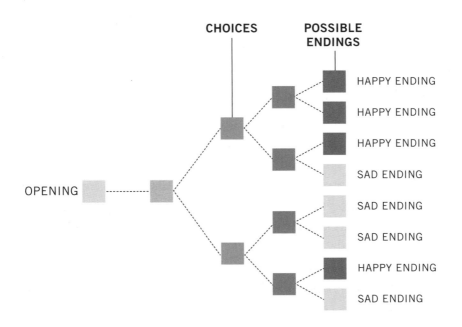

There is a production problem with multiple story paths in actual video games, however. Content creation (art, animation, sound effects, scripting) costs money, and there's a very hard-to-resist argument that says "if we're spending all this money creating game levels and such, why would you create story paths where players might miss a lot of it?"

There's also a problem with multiple endings. If you have to play through 40 hours of a game to get to one of several big narrative payoffs, you're going to want to make certain you're going to see "The Good One." So if a game features alternative endings, developers tend to make those endings similar but for a few little details, so as not to disappoint players who don't feel like spending another 40 hours just to see an alternate ending. Some games, however, feature wildly different endings, often tied to "moral" choices you as a player make throughout the story of the game.

Even branching middles can present dilemmas for players, especially for "completists" like Bob who feel compelled to talk to all the NPCs, collect all the collectibles, and see all the side quests in a game. Early in *Fallout 3*, for example, you (as the Vault Dweller) are asked to make a moral choice: whether to save or nuke the nearby town of Megaton. The nuclear explosion is spectacular—all the way down to the blast wave you feel via the force feedback buzzer in the game controller—but it's only experienced by "bad" players who choose to nuke the defenseless little town. In order to play down both paths, you either have to replay the game entirely or create a lot of save files so that you can reload just before a critical decision point and choose the road not yet taken.

Many neophyte game writers love the exciting storytelling possibilities that video games hold. But what they don't understand is that we are still learning the rules of branching narrative. The number of people who want to *write* IF is, to date, far, far larger than those who want to *read* IF. We don't yet have that IF masterwork that will bring thousands of new IF readers. We do know that *good* branching narrative uses player choices to shape their experience in a meaningful way—one that resonates with the theme of the work or which evokes an emotional response. If you recall, however fondly, reading back and forth in the old Choose Your Own Adventure books was fun, but not necessarily meaningful. It had the feeling of opening all the boxes in an advent calendar all at once. It didn't matter what the rules were, you just wanted to see what was in there.

In our experience, the best way to understand the delights and challenges of branching narrative is to explore and create in the world of interactive fiction, where there are good free tools and a growing body of very good content to study. We'll discuss some of the tools in a later chapter, but a great portal for IF content is Emily Short's Interactive Storytelling (https://emshort.wordpress.com). Ms. Short is, in our opinion, the doyenne of IF and her blog is the center of a very lively worldwide community of creators and fans.

Non-Linear Narrative

There is a long tradition of excellent movies that play with the rules of linear narrative, subverting the audience's expectation of a straight shot through the story and presenting instead repetition (*Rashomon*), inversion (*Betrayal*), both (*Memento*), simultaneity (*Timecode*), and shuffling (*Pulp Fiction*).

Game design lends itself very easily to the creation of stories in which players "follow their noses." So-called "open world" or "sandbox" games are designed to seem like you can play what you want, where you want, when you want.

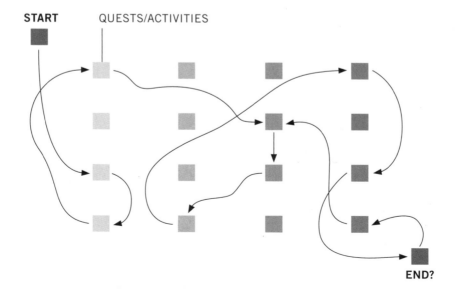

Such games may not use a traditional three-act structure as a whole, but their component missions tend to. Many role-playing games (*Skyrim, Dragon Age*) have a linear main story line, but you do not have to follow it, or even finish it, in order to play the game. You are free to explore the world and discover multiple side quests and missions to play. *Dragon Age: Inquisition* has over 125 hours of additional content. That is more time than the entire run of *The Sopranos*, more time than all seven *Star Wars* movies, and all of the shared-universe Marvel movies so far—combined!

TIME IS DIFFERENT IN VIDEO GAMES

We've heard screenwriting compared to freestyle swimming in a lap pool. You can do whatever you want to do, within general limits: most features run about two hours, sitcoms are about a half hour, and "Gross! How'd he die?" forensics shows are about one hour. The rule of thumb for screenwriting, and the reason scripts follow a strict format on the page, is that one page of script is equal to one minute of screen time.

Movies are balanced. Act One will run about 30 pages or 30 minutes. The last act will be about the same: 30 minutes. And the middle of the movie will about 60 minutes with the midpoint coming 30 minutes in. These are general guidelines, as not all movies are the same length, but movie structure tends to even out over the length of the film.

A television pilot is essentially the first act of a television series with the bulk of the series being Act Two. Thirty minutes to set up a story? You betcha. Which is why most TV pilots: (a) introduce the characters, (b) ask a lot of questions, and (c) posit questions that the series is going to have to answer. Will they get off the island? *Gilligan's Island* or *Lost*. When will he put on the tights? *Smallville*. Who killed Laura Palmer? *Twin Peaks*. These are often called the "engines" that drive the television series. A series needs an engine that will generate weekly stories, which is why procedurals (police, law, medical) are always so popular with TV writers and execs. Set a story in a hospital and incoming patients = incoming stories. Video games need "engines" also.

The engine of *The Last of* Us is to get Ellie to the Fireflies. That drives the story. Structurally, movies and television shows have a narrative balance where the first act might be the same length as the third. Twenty-five minutes of Act One in a movie will probably be balanced by about twenty-five minutes of Act Three. Video game narrative is not balanced. For example, the first act of *The Last of Us* takes only about twenty-five minutes of game time. The rest of the game takes many hours to complete. *Fallout 3* uses the player character's childhood in the vault as the tutorial to fill the players in on the premise, as well as to show them the basic mechanics of the game. We learn very quickly in *God of War* that Kratos wants revenge against Ares (he is the dragon who must be slain). But it takes hours of gameplay to learn *why* he wants revenge. It's a pretty good reveal. Play it.

In similar manner, games with a day-night cycle typically don't take 12 real hours to move from day to night. In *Jak and Daxter: The Precursor Legacy*, for example, the lighting scheme changes depending upon what time of "day" it was, but an in-game day lasts only a few minutes. Playing through a level would take a completetist gamer "days" even though less than an hour would have passed in real life.

THE "SLAY THE DRAGON" STRUCTURE

Why is it so important to have a structure? When writing a screenplay, we always begin with the structure so we know where we are going as storytellers and know where the characters are going as people (and yes, stories about talking fish or cute aliens or janky robots are always, ultimately, about people). The audience connection to *Wall-E*: Loneliness. Making a connection. You have to know the end of the game to know how to get there. Even when a medium can have multiple endings, you have to know where to begin.

Here are some core *Slay the Dragon* principles of structure that we believe are crucial to writing a good interactive story. We designed it as a pyramid and call it the Pyra-Grid, because games start small and then go big.

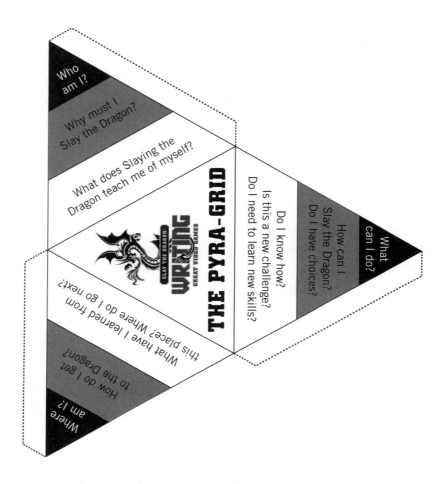

Interactive narrative is 3D storytelling, so it helps to visualize game structure in three dimensions. (Make a photocopy of this page, cut out the Pyra-Grid, fold along the base, and add a little glue along the tabs.) By thinking about the game as a whole, a level, a mission, or even a non-interactive scene along these three dimensions, it helps you make certain that your story and the gameplay are moving along. You could even use multiple Pyra-Grids for different characters or groups of characters in your game.

A NO-ACT STRUCTURE?

At the 2014 Game Developers Conference, Riot Games's Tom Abernathy and Richard Rouse III, the design lead for Microsoft Game Studios, presented a panel entitled "Death to the Three-Act Structure! Toward a Unique Structure for Game Narratives." They argued that "Games stories are *not* Structure." Their thesis concludes that *character* and *user experience* are more important.[40]

We totally agree, and yet we disagree.

They have stumbled on a crucial dilemma that all writers face: which is more important, *plot* or *character*?

It is both.

<u>*Plot is there so the character* can change.</u>

You need plot. You need characters running around in your plot. Structure is what you use to craft the story so the character(s) has somewhere to go, something to do and ultimately can change. Develop. Improve. Embiggen. Even if you make your characters die, they should die feeling comforted that their life meant something, or that they die wiser than they lived. This is why we want our characters to progress— to "arc"—as people, just as we as players want our abilities to increase and our challenges to grow.

The "no-act" structure for us means there is no set structure for a video game. There is no paradigm. There is no one-size-fits-all. But there *is* a *structure*.

There are many successful story structures to choose from.

There are many great stories to learn from. There are many games to play to see how those creators told their story. Games and interactive fiction need not conform to structural rules the way most Hollywood scripts do. Games as a medium are still evolving and finding a path (pun intended), much as television evolved from movies and movies evolved from stage drama.

If the player or viewer doesn't care about what happens to the hero, then it doesn't matter how well-structured the game, movie, or TV show is.

So maybe it's time to meet the protagonist. And in the world of video games, that protagonist is you. The PC! The player-character.

---

40 http://www.gdcvault.com/play/1020050/Death-to-the-Three-Act

Speaking of Structure

1 EXPRESS THE QUEST IN ONE LINE

In your Game Journal, list ten games that you've played or that you're familiar with. Next to each title, write one sentence that states the main objective of that game. What does the player want? What does the PC want? What is the engine that drives the narrative forward? Why is the PC having trouble getting what he wants?

Remember, your purpose here is not to summarize the plot. It is simply to distill into one line the main quest of the game, and why that quest is difficult.

2 REVERSE ENGINEER A GAME STORY

Play a game (or watch a game movie). Write down the major story points. Can you identify a three-act structure? A five-act structure? Any structure? Can you see the *whammos*—the big moments that spin the story in a new direction?

Screenwriting students do this sort of thing all the time with movies. It's not as common for game developers to do, but they should.

3 REBOOT A CLASSIC GAME

Take an old classic arcade game or a mobile game that is light on story. Can it be "rebooted" as a story-driven game? Can you change the genre? For example, could you rework Pac-Man as a survival horror game? Who is Pac-Man? What have Inky, Blinky, Pinky, and Clyde become?

4 STRUCTURE YOUR GAME

You've been working on the story of Your Game for some time now. Let's break that story down a couple of ways.

In one sentence, write down the main action of the story of Your Game, as you did in the first exercise.

Now expand that one sentence to one paragraph: Make sure you have a beginning, middle, and end using a very *linear narrative*.

Finally, let's rework it. Take the same scenario and, using hyperlinks (in Word, Pages, or Google Docs), create a *branching narrative* with different paths and varying outcomes. It can be any of the structures discussed in this chapter. So for your example, you might write that the character is confronted with going through a cave, or over a mountain. Each decision will lead to a different scenario.

You could also use inklewriter (www.inklestudios.com/inklewriter), which is a free browser-based tool for writing interactive fiction. We'll discuss inklewriter more toward the end of the book, but it's so simple to use that you can get started now.

CHAPTER 05

Writing a Great Playable Character

THE EVOLUTION OF THE VIDEO GAME CHARACTER

There exists a long tradition of meatheaded video game protagonists like *Duke Nukem* who owe their existence to the popularity of 1980s "shoot first, ask questions later" action movie heroes played by Sylvester Stallone, Arnold Schwarzenegger, and Chuck Norris. There were exceptions, such as Mario and Ms. Pac-Man, but it seems as though the default setting for many games was a Reagan-era white male action hero.

Part of it was the American *zeitgeist* of the time. As video games emerged as a narrative medium in the '80s and early '90s, much of pop culture—eager to shake off post-Vietnam and post-Watergate disillusionment—was obsessed with fables of male power: the *Rambo* movies, the *Missing in Action* movies, *Commando, Predator, Die Hard*. On TV, *Miami Vice*. In the comics, with *The Dark Knight Returns*, Batman was made over (or finally revealed) as an angry sociopath. Marvel's most popular superhero at the time, Wolverine, was a short, angry, Canadian sociopath. And don't get us started on the Punisher.

As game developers either licensed these movies directly or created similar characters so that players could feel like Stallone's Rambo character (in *Contra*) or any Chuck Norris character (in *River City Rampage*), there was a very homogeneous quality to a big swath of game heroes. Action trumped story, and Duke Nukem became the Steven Seagal of video games. (Jean-Claude Van Damme became the Jean-Claude Van Damme of video games when he starred in the *Street Fighter* movie.) Character did not matter. He had a gun. He had a target. He had an audience. This hyper-macho, action-über-alles attitude has been reprised with ironic humor in Stallone's *Expendables* movie franchise and in developer Free Lives' game *Broforce*.

In many American games, protagonists were often angry loners or super-competent operatives into whose shoes players could jump, climb, fight, and shoot, then hear themselves utter a cool line, like "Guess again, freakshow. I'm coming back to town, and the last thing that's gonna go through your mind before you die . . . is my size-13 boot!" (*Duke Nukem 3D*). This reflected the fact that clearing the level was no big deal; it was all in a day's work for the PC. These were men of action, whose emotions ranged across a very narrow spectrum, from anger to cool cynicism—the very spectrum that is the tiny emotional comfort zone of teenage boys.

In Japanese games of the same era, protagonists were very often actual teenage boys. Bewildered by the fantastic situations they would find themselves in, quick to anger, and only very reluctantly accepting of the fact that the world needed them to step up and fulfill their destiny (e.g., to grow up), the typical Japanese game protagonist of the time (like *Final Fantasy VII*'s Cloud Strife) was designed to be as relatable as possible to its target audience—angsty teenage boys (and girls!).

If a story is a journey of emotion, the journey in these early American games seemed very short.

Who Is Tabula Rosa?

Game developers have another tendency—making their hero a blank slate. One of the hoariest clichés in video games is that of the Amnesiac Protagonist who is:

- a tabula rasa onto whom players can map their own emotions, and
- unaware of his or her own abilities within the game (like the player).

We believe that many players no longer want Tabula Rosa, or her brother Tabula Ross. Entering into the shoes of an actual character makes for a more emotionally involving play experience. Screenwriters and playwrights are trained to show only the tip of an iceberg when it comes to character. There is a lot more going on underneath the surface of the water that we never get to see: the backstory. Quirks. Points of view. Games were developed from the tech outward—there was never a need to see more of a backstory. Mario is a plumber. Duke likes to blow things up.

Take a quick glance at the evolution of Mario—how deep could characters be when they were so low tech? Look at the *Prince of Persia*—same game, different platforms. We have come a long way from programmers writing dialogue for 16-bit 2D characters. Jordan Mechner originally created *Prince of Persia* from the game mechanics outward. Yes, the Prince had an objective, but he did not have much of an arc. How could he?

As the years passed, Mechner moved from writing the code for the games to focusing on their stories. As the graphics became three-dimensional, he made the Prince more three-dimensional. In modern versions of the game (starting with 2003's *Prince of Persia: The Sands of Time*), you play as the Prince for hours and hours. You want him to be interesting. You want to go along on his emotional journey as well as his journey of action.

A-List Talent Demands A-List Roles

We are now in an era wherein game producers cast actors not just to voice the characters from a game, but to capture their performance so that they bring their characters to life. In *L.A. Noire*, the characters played by Aaron Staton (TV's *Mad Men*) and John Noble (*The Lord of the Rings: The Return of the King*, TV's *Fringe*, and *Sleepy Hollow*) not only sound like Aaron Staton and John Noble, but they *look* and *emote* like Aaron Staton and John Noble. Major talent agencies like William Morris Endeavor and CAA are fielding offers for their acting clients to appear in games. Creative directors, writers, and gameplay designers are no longer just making doll-like avatars that you move around the screen with your controller—they are writing true *characters*.

And this evolution is slowly getting the medium recognized as an art form. The British Academy of Film and Television Arts (BAFTA) is the UK's equivalent of our Academy of Motion Picture Arts and Sciences. In 2002, BAFTA began to host the BAFTA Games Awards, honoring winners in categories such as Best Game, Best Design, and Best Game Innovation. In 2005, they added screenplay but then later renamed it Best Story. In 2011, they added the category of Best Digital Performer.

Here's just a small sample of A-list actors who've performed in games:

Sean Bean	*Malcolm McDowell*
Kristen Bell	*Liam Neeson*
Stephen Fry	*Ellen Page*
Ricky Gervais	*Hayden Panettiere*
Jeff Goldblum	*Ron Perlman*
John Goodman	*Andy Serkis*
Heather Graham	*Martin Sheen*
Neil Patrick Harris	*Kevin Spacey*
Linda Hunt	*Patrick Stewart*
Samuel L. Jackson	*Yvonne Strahovski*
Ben Kingsley	*Kiefer Sutherland*
Ray Liotta	*Elijah Wood*

And this is just a partial list. There are Oscar nominees and winners, Tony-award winners, stars of popular TV shows and movies who have been adored by critics and audiences. What's attracting all this great talent? It's not the money, and the fact that they can blow things up (they can do that in movies, too).

It's the *characters*. It always starts with the characters.

Or does it?

WRITING FROM THE ARC BACKWARDS

What is more important in a story—the plot or the characters? Is it plot? Well, sure, that makes sense—no one wants to watch or play something boring. No one likes a story that "doesn't go anywhere." Think about it:

the world, the action, the promise of the adventure—that's the movie poster, that's the trailer running on ginormous screens at E3. That's the game box! But what about characters? Brad Pitt, Reese Witherspoon, Denzel Washington, name almost any respected actor or actress and they'll tell you that they're not just interested in being in a good story, but that they want to inhabit the lives of challenging and conflicted characters.

A good story should result in the main character undergoing some sort of emotional transformation, or *character arc*. A story is a journey of emotion and a game is a journey of action. How do we combine the two to create a transference of emotion so that the player does not just play the game but experiences the emotions of the character? Stay tuned for our next chapter! But first, we need to break down what makes a good character—in a game, a movie, or any type of story.

In most stories, the plot is a vehicle that drives the protagonist to change. You want a story line (action) that impacts the character line (emotion). An engaging game or movie or television show has a story line that exposes the character's flaw(s), makes her confront her fears and leads to an arc. If your story is not forcing *change* on the character, then either the story is wrong, or the character is wrong. The *actions* of the story impact the *emotion* of the story.

Know Thy Ending!

Good dramatic writing is done backwards. To develop a strong emotional impact, the writer needs to know—*in any story, for any platform*—what the ending is! You have to know where you are going if you want to get there. And for a story to work, to deeply involve the player and the audience, the writer has to know how the main character is going to change.

Writer! Know thy ending! If you don't know where you're going, how do you know where to start? Who is the protagonist at the beginning of the story? What has he or she become at the end of the story?

In *Titanic*, Rose (played by Kate Winslet) goes from a sheltered, pampered rich kid to an adventurous young woman who lives her life to the fullest. In *Avatar,* Jake Sully (actor Sam Worthington) is an emotionally burned-out ex-Marine who, by the end of the story, is the passionate leader of a revolution. In the original *Terminator,* Sarah Connor (played by Linda Hamilton) transforms from a naïve waitress to the selfless defender of humanity. In *Terminator 2: Judgment Day,* the Terminator changes from a machine to a father-like machine who sacrifices himself for the humans he has grown to love. OK, those are all James Cameron characters. (We were on a roll.) Let's look at some others. We offer up Shrek, Nemo's dad Marlin, Belle (and Sebastian), Ariel, Luke Skywalker, Han Solo, and Michael Corleone.

The "all characters must change" rule, like all rules, has some exceptions. Indiana Jones and James Bond come to mind; there's not much of an emotional journey beyond "I was a loner, but now I have a girlfriend/dad/sidekick who will be long gone by the next picture." Danny Ocean (George Clooney) and Rusty Ryan (Brad Pitt) don't arc much from one movie to the next in the *Ocean's Eleven* franchise—nor, if we're being honest, do we want them to. (They do get a wife and a girlfriend, though.)

If you want to write a great video game, create a character that goes on a journey of change. The journey of action should influence and affect the journey of emotion. So how do video games bring change to the player character?

What Do Kratos and Michael Corleone Have in Common?

You want a character who doesn't merely grow more powerful over time. (Almost all player characters are designed to do this. Players want greater abilities, then greater challenges to test those abilities.) You want a character that emotionally transforms as well. One of the most iconic characters in American pop culture history is Michael Corleone (portrayed by Al Pacino) in *The Godfather.* We meet Michael when he attends his sister's wedding. He tells his girlfriend, Kate (Diane Keaton), that he is nothing like his family of criminal royalty. In the original *God of War,* Kratos is also a hero of sorts. He is a warrior bound in service to the Greek gods. What does the world of ancient Greece have in common with the world of the Mafia in post–WW II New York?

Both men are anti-heroes. They are not on the typical hero's journey. They are conflicted. They both hate the place they ultimately end up.

Michael does not wish to be the Godfather. His wish (and his father's wish) was that Michael would lead the family away from crime and toward American legitimacy. Kratos wants to kill himself. He wants to be free of his life of fighting and of guilt-ridden rage for what he was tricked into doing. (SPOILER: He killed his own family.)

Both men become that which they despise. Both characters are constructed from their destination backwards. The writers built the ending into the characters. They each have a character arc. Michael doesn't want to become his father, but he does. Kratos wants to kill Ares, yet he takes Ares' place as the God of War. A story where a mafia son wants to follow in his father's footsteps and be the big boss himself is not much of a story. It conforms to our expectations; good stories challenge our expectations. This is why Michael's older brother Sonny (James Caan) is not the focus of the movie. You want your protagonist to have the most emotional distance to cover over the course of the story. Your main character's arc should be long.

We think games are better with strong protagonists and carefully constructed character arcs. We like to summarize an arc with this concentrated sentence. Call it a formula. Call it a cheat sheet. Call it the Five C's of Character.

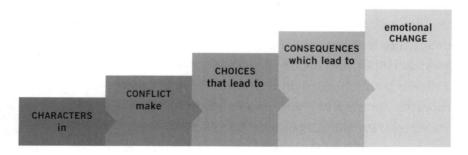

As you develop your main character, or choose your main character, flesh him or her out with these five C's. We don't want to play as an ordinary thimble or shoe. We want to know who that thimble really is. What its hopes and dreams are. What was its most severe childhood trauma?

So let's start by examining character. Who am I when playing this game? Why am I here? What do I *want*? What do I *need*? One side of the Pyra-Grid.

Characters

You want to create characters that have the largest emotional distance to travel in the story. Alfred Hitchcock, the Master of Suspense, had this formula for creating a suspense thriller. Again and again, he made movies about ordinary people in extraordinary situations. You should contrast your character against the backdrop of the world in which your game is taking place and give him or her the harshest time possible. Remember the quote from *Repo Man*. Your job is to get your character into tense situations. And lots of them.

Dead Space was a best-selling game that launched a franchise. Heavily influenced by the movie *Alien*, it is the story of Isaac Clarke, a "systems engineer" (maintenance man), who has to use his skills to make weapons and survive the attack of monstrous space zombies on his ship. Isaac is not a warrior. He is a not a military genius. He is a regular guy who has to survive by his wits. He is the most likely candidate to die first—yet he survives.

Assassin's Creed's main character, Desmond Miles, is a bartender who is forced by multinational conglomerate Abstergo Industries to interact with the Animus (a time machine for the mind), and travel into the genetic memories of his ancestors. Interesting. But imagine if Desmond was a spy, a hit-man, or other murderous criminal who then has to travel into his memories. It would be no big deal, we think. That scenario would meet our expectations. But a bartender who has to learn how to be an assassin? That's a long stretch. But a more interesting one.

In *Infamous*, Cole MacGrath is a bike messenger who develops super powers. Eddie Riggs is a roadie who has to go to Hell and back in *Brütal Legend*. In *BioShock,* you play as Jack, a Hitchcockian every-man. Andrew Ryan believes you have been sent to kill him, so he tries to kill you first. *Alan Wake* is a confused novelist in the game of the same name. Lee Everett is an average college professor in Telltale Games' *The

Walking Dead. Not a professor of zombie slaying; that would be too easy. His former career is useless in the new world of the Walkers. Why? *It's more dramatic that way!*

The Ordinary Meets the Extraordinary

Lord of the Rings should not only be viewed as the precursor to *Dungeons & Dragons*. It is also the primer for an ordinary man in extraordinary situations. In a world of Orcs, Dwarves, Elves, Wizards, talking trees, and eagles the size of a Greyhound bus, the bravest and the one who leads the journey is a humble, home-loving Hobbit—the one character most like us.

That is the empathy a player is looking for and a storyteller in any medium should aim to achieve. Hollywood types call this "relatability."

"What if this happened to me?" the movie audience thinks. "This is really happening to me!" the game players think.

We relate to characters who, like us, aren't perfect. The more screwed-up a person is, the more human we recognize him to be, the more relatable. If you want characters to be more "realistic," make them screw up. Give them fears and prejudices. Make them *flawed*.

WHO'S MORE AWESOME, SUPERMAN OR BATMAN?

Who's more awesome: Superman or Batman? G'ahead. Take some time to think about this. Not who's more powerful . . . who's the more compelling *character*? The more interesting one. Who is the one who has the clear emotional drive that informs every decision he makes?

The answer is, of course, The Batman.

Why? Well, he's a human being—we can relate to that. Superman is a gifted alien—he's always been an *Übermensch*—literally an "Overman"— above us mere mortals. The other thing that holds Supes back from being a great character: *he has no flaws*, other than being kind of a stiff. He's the Boy Scout from Space. (Batman, meanwhile, is the Angry Obsessive from Gotham City.)

Superman does not get hurt. He always does the right thing. Ma and Pa Kent did a very good job raising him, and in every version of

Superman's childhood they tell him he has been put on this earth for a reason. When Superman first appears in comic books, there was no Kryptonite; that was added years later on his radio show as his writers realized that he had no weaknesses. With no weaknesses, there was no chance of dying, no chance of failure, and hence *no drama*. Pre-Kryptonite Superman was incapable of getting into a tense situation. You (and he) always knew that he would triumph.

Batman is human, mortal. Batman can get hurt. We can relate to that. Even though he's got lots of cool gadgets—and is in way better shape than us—we wince every time he takes a punch. Not so with Supes. (Does he even feel pain?)

Batman also has emotional issues, and he wears them on his sleeve. He saw his parents murdered, and was raised by an elderly British man, Alfred, alone in a Gothic mansion. That kind of trauma can mess you up. Superman's parents were killed, too, but he didn't witness it. He was raised in a loving two-parent home in Kansas, and the Kents waited until Clark was a teenager to tell him he was adopted.

Superman is the quintessential good citizen, student council president, altar boy. He's the kid in school your mother always compared you less favorably to.

Batman is not. In some ways he is a psychopath. He's still working out his childhood trauma. For our sake, let's hope he always does.

Also—and this is important—Superman is inherently *passive*, while Batman is inherently *active*. Superman didn't choose to come to Earth; he was sent here by his father. He didn't choose to be raised by the Kents; he was found by them and raised with their Midwestern All-American values. Very little of what makes classic Superman Superman is based on his own choices. (Ma Kent even designed his costume!)

Batman, however, created his own persona. He chose to dedicate himself to fighting crime, chose to enter a years-long regimen of brutal physical training and eye-crossing scientific study. He puts himself at mortal risk every night, patrolling the streets of Gotham, trying to rid the city of criminals. (Yes, he had the advantage of inheriting a fortune from his murdered parents. However, at no point in over seven decades of the Batman mythos does Bruce Wayne *ever* hint that his wealth was worth the price he paid for it.)

Well-crafted characters are *flawed*. Which is to say, good characters are like us. Think about it: *Seinfeld, Dexter, Lost, Gone Girl, Breaking Bad, Girls, Transparent, Iron Man, Spider-Man, Citizen Kane*—all feature characters who have major flaws.

Let's go further back: Hamlet, Othello, King Lear, Macbeth, Romeo, Juliet. All the memorable characters of literature and drama. The ones who stick to the wall. The ones who've been written to our collective hard drives. They're all—in ways great and small—not quite right in the head.

It's more interesting watching imperfect people flail around than watching perfect people execute perfectly.

We relate to mistakes, miscues, misunderstandings, vanity (or any of the other seven deadly sins). We relate to people screwing up. (Search for "fail" on YouTube when you have several days to kill.) We identify with losers much more often than winners.

Because human beings are not omniscient, we're all insecure, afraid, imperfect. We like seeing characters with similar insecurities struggle and overcome obstacles. It gives us hope for our own screwed-up lives.

Where do these flaws originate?

CONFLICT: THE ESSENCE OF DRAMA

One of the best places to begin developing a flawed character is to develop an *internal conflict*. Internal conflict comes from an emotional dilemma that results in the opposition of *want* and *need*. What a character wants and what a character needs should be at war with each other. Characters are going to deal with external conflicts later, throughout your story. That's the journey-of-action part of the game. External conflict is everything that is placed in the character's path as he or she attempts to achieve their goals. Hordes of the Geth, green pigs, Koopa Troopas, giant spiders, falling bridges, mind-bending puzzles—these are all external, and they're easy to create. The trick is to create an *internal conflict* for your hero(ine). That's the stuff that makes them interesting.

Luke Skywalker *wants* to be a space pilot. He *needs* to stop saying things like, "I'll never" and "I can't."

Jack in *BioShock wants* to escape Rapture. He *needs* to learn how to make his own choices, which fits perfectly with the whole mind control "Would You Kindly" theme playing out in that story.

Jack in *The Last of Us wants* to be left alone. He *needs* to be a parent again. So let's stick him with a substitute for his dead daughter.

The Vault Dweller, hero of *Fallout 3, wants* to find his father but *needs* to learn to survive on his (or her) own outside the warped society of Vault 101. It's coming of age in the post-apocalypse.

BACKSTORY: HOW IS *FINDING NEMO* LIKE *THE LAST OF US*?

Internal conflict can also come from the *backstory* of a character. A character might be haunted by something that happened to him or her in the past. This event that forges who the character is has been used in cinema, literature, and theater countless times for dramatic effect. The backstory is the "ghost" that haunts our protagonist and helps to explain why they're so messed up. In the Batman stories, the ghost is that primal scene, flashed back to again and again, of the murder of Bruce Wayne's parents. In *Hamlet* the ghost is an actual ghost—that of Hamlet's father.

There is no one correct and only way to reveal this "ghost," but it's almost always some type of traumatic loss or failure. The ghost might be played out early in the story (again, see *Hamlet*), in a second-act flashback (every other movie you've ever seen), or it might only be hinted at and never made explicit (see *Chinatown*). Hitchcock's *Vertigo* opens with Scottie (Jimmy Stewart) unable to save a policeman from falling to his death. In *Jaws*, it is just before the end of the second act when we learn that Quint (Robert Shaw) harbors a mortal fear of sharks that stems from one very bad day in the Navy.

Speaking of things nautical, in *Finding Nemo*, we see Nemo's dad Marlin (voiced by Albert Brooks) lose his wife Coral and their hundreds of fertilized eggs to a barracuda. At the end of this sad beginning, Marlin finds only one egg is left: Nemo's. Marlin promises his unborn son that he'll never let anything bad happen to him.

Story-driven video games also use "ghosts" as backstory. We've already mentioned *God of War*: in the middle of the game we learn that Kratos murdered his own family. In *The Last of Us,* the game opens with a combination of narration and cut scenes that can only be called a prequel. We first see Joel as a loving dad until the mutated strain of the *Cordyceps* fungus causes the world to descend into madness and his daughter Sarah is murdered in front of him. (Are you seeing a pattern here? Lots of witnessed murder—few things are more traumatic.) The story then cuts to years later where the ghost of that fateful day influences every decision and narrative choice that Joel, the player character, makes. The end of the game's story is set up in those first few moments.

Jack (*BioShock*), Geralt (*The Witcher*), and Samantha Greenbriar (*Gone Home*) are all characters whose backstory comes into play in the game's narrative. On the airplane in the very beginning of *BioShock*, Jack (you) looks at family photos. These come back into your notice through the game. As the story unfolds you gradually learn your shocking backstory: you are the illegitimate son of the man who now wants to kill you—Andrew Ryan.

Booker DeWitt (*BioShock Infinite*) is an emotionally scarred, disgraced detective. Does his backstory come into play? You bet it does. In *Red Dead Redemption*, you play as John Marston, whose life as an outlaw has led to your being recruited for a mission that starts the main story line. Keeping it primal, John has to kill the members of his old gang in order to save his family.

Of course, exceptions abound. They do in every medium. There is no one way to do a thing. (And in good game design, it's better if the player has more than one way to solve a problem.) Not all characters change. Sometimes the circumstances around them change, but characters might be clearly defined and stay that way through the series. Nathan Drake does not change much in the *Uncharted* games. He does not have a deep inner wounded soul. (Neither did Indiana Jones.) It seems to have worked out fine for both of them. On most police procedurals, the main characters will not have much of an emotional journey in an episode. But over the course of a season, or an entire series, they will tend to evolve—often in spite of themselves. (See Dennis Franz' Lt. Sipowicz on *NYPD Blue*.)

DON'T TELL BOWSER:
THE BAD GUYS THINK IT'S THEIR GAME

When we think about some of the greatest, most memorable and dynamic characters, we might not always have the protagonist in mind. The story of Adam and Eve features the Serpent, who's the most interesting character (as he introduces . . . conflict! Also Sin and Man's Fall, which is kind of a bummer as well, but definitely dramatic). After that, Cain takes center stage. Then God himself in the form of the Flood.

Literature and drama are filled with antagonists who, as has often been said about Lady Macbeth, steal the show. Moby Dick. Mr. Hyde. Iago. Hannibal Lecter, Darth Vader, the shark in *Jaws*—evil, evil, evil. (Fun fact: Iago has more lines in *Othello* than the title character. Watch Iago in action and try not to think of Kevin Spacey's Frank Underwood in the American version of *House of Cards*.)

One of our mantras, that we have repeated to each other for years, is that a story is only as good as its villain. And if you want to create a good villain, you should understand that he or she thinks they are the stars of the show; the hero of the game. This is true of good stories with good antagonists—and remember that an antagonist need not be actually tie-her-to-the-railroad-tracks evil (though it helps). Their only requirement is that their *want* and Our Hero(ine)'s *want* are mutually exclusive. They conflict. "There can be only one!" One of the most memorable not-evil antagonists in cinema is U.S. Marshal Samuel Gerard (Tommy Lee Jones) in *The Fugitive*. His relentless pursuit of wrongly-convicted escapee Dr. Richard Kimble (Harrison Ford) forms the spine of that movie. The so-called One-Armed Man who really killed Kimble's wife—the actual bad guy—pales in comparison.

You should use the same tenets in creating your villain as we discussed above in creating your hero(ine). What do they *want*? What do they *need*? How do those objectives conflict?

Yes, the book is called *Slay the Dragon*. And yes, the villain might be a dragon. But that Dragon does not know he's a villain. If your game story is about a White Knight having to rescue a princess from a Dragon's lair, then the Dragon thinks the game story is about a human invading his home: a human who is destroying his habitat with cheaply built McCastles on cleared forest land that once supported his diet of deer, boars, and bears. To the Dragon, *the white knight is the bad guy*! You have to be able to see the game through the villain's story. (If you haven't already seen *Wreck-It Ralph*, put this book down and find it. Watch it. It's the perfect example of a story told from the "villain's" point of view. And it was a huge hit!)

Portal features GLaDOS (Genetic Lifeform and Disk Operating System), a manipulative, sociopathic AI whose job is to test a human subject, Chell. Mario's nemesis, Wario, proved so popular he's starred in two of his own game series, *Wario Land* and *WarioWare*. Death (yes, *that* Death) is actually the "hero" of *Darksiders II*. Andrew Ryan in *BioShock* is a business magnate who leads a horde of mutant "splicers" to protect his fallen Utopia. He's an iconic character based on none other than Howard Hughes, Ayn Rand, and Walt Disney.[41]

Do all games have villains? In some form, yes. A game without obstacles is not a game; those obstacles are personified by villains. They might be impersonal, like the environment-as-antagonist game *Limbo,* or personal, like Bowser showing up to steal Princess Peach in *Super Mario Bros*. Let's don't forget the smug, taunting green pigs in *Angry Birds*. From space zombies in *Dead Space* to land zombies in . . . practically any other survival horror game, *someone* should be trying to stop the player character from slaying the Dragon.

———

AND THE DRAGON GOES TO: THE BEST SUPPORTING NPC

As the player character (the PC) wanders through a game—either on a main quest, or playing in the sandbox of an open world—he or she will encounter *non-player characters* (NPCs). These are placed in the game to provide clues, backstory, direction, hints, companionship, or even comic relief. The NPCs help bring the game world to life.

There has been a tendency among game developers, especially with games adapted from other media, to make a game's strongest characters into NPCs, and let the PC act alongside (or on behalf of) them. You remember the sociopathic NPC GLaDOS from *Portal*, not the mute PC Chell. In *The Godfather: The Game*, the PC begins as a very minor player in the Corleone organization. You don't play as Vito or Michael Corleone—though you get to meet and take orders from Vito. In *Star Wars: The Force Unleashed*, you are Starkiller, billed as "Darth Vader's

41 http://www.rockpapershotgun.com/2007/08/20/exclusive-ken-levine-on-the-making-of-bioshock/

secret apprentice," but you don't play as Darth Vader (except in the tutorial level).

Good characters frustrate and surprise us. They always have (*Hamlet*), and continue to do so (Walter White, Don Draper). Video game protagonists are catching up. For a long time, the NPCs might be the most interesting characters on the screen. The recent *Assassin's Creed: Unity* boasts of ten thousand individualized NPCs. Ellie in *The Last of Us* is an NPC for most of the game, but takes over the action when Joel is hurt. The NPCs are the supporting cast. They build up the protagonist. They challenge the hero on his or her journey of action.

Meeting Your Characters

1 REMEMBER YOUR FAVORITE CHARACTERS

Write down your five favorite video game characters. What is their backstory? What is their goal? What do you like about them? (Be specific. Answers like "she's cool" or "he's bad-ass" don't help you at all.) What traits do they have? Write down a one-line description of each character.

Now, maybe even more importantly, in the same game, who is their antagonist? Who or what are the main obstacles holding the hero at bay? The pigs in *Angry Birds*. The Reapers of *Mass Effect*. Write down a one-line description of the protagonist's antagonist.

2 MAKE CHARACTER CREATION CARDS

On ten index cards, list *ten ordinary professions*. Something we all might have the ability to become: teacher, policeman, fireman, waiter, trucker, professor, scientist. Not super hero or galactic bounty hunter. Now you might say, "I want my character to be a bad-ass fireman!" First of all, we told you not to use "bad-ass," because it's not specific (and a cliché). *Give them a flaw.* An "arrogant fireman with something to prove," is inherently more interesting than a "bad-ass" because we recognize (and empathize with) insecurity. Commander Shepherd in *Mass Effect* is arrogant and is also the first human to join the Spectres. Insecure? Oh, yes!

On ten more index cards, list *ten character archetypes*. There are many different archetypes you can use, but we want to avoid such overused tropes as "man out for revenge," or "bad-ass space marine," or "amnesiac loner." (Wait a second, you might say: you just described the characters from *God of War, Halo,* and *Silent Hill.* Yes, but the writers of those stories spin the tropes on their heads.) Let's instead use the planets of our solar system as our archetypes. (Include Pluto and either the sun or the moon to get to an even ten.) Think about what traits might be associated with each planet. For example, to us, Venus conjures up mist and love and warmth. Mars evokes feelings of battle and rage. Neptune is cool. Mercury is quick. You may have very different associations. But use those impressions as the basis of your character's archetypes, one per card.

Take a final set of ten cards and list *ten extraordinary situations.* Your hero time travels to an ancient Rome where humans are enslaved by an alien race. He goes into hell to try to kill Satan. She crash-lands in the middle of a sub-Saharan civil war and has to choose sides.

Shuffle the cards of each type: profession, archetype, and situation. Keep them in three separate stacks. Then mix and match cards from each of the stacks. What did you come up with? Keep at it until you have a combination that really excites you.

Finally, write in three sentences how the extraordinary situation will force your main character to change. Who will they become by the end of the story? Does your bossy Jupiter learn to play nice with others?

CHAPTER 06

WHO AM I WHEN I PLAY?
GAMEPLAY AS METHOD ACTING

PLAYING YOUR CHARACTER

Let's play Monopoly! Do you want to be the Top Hat? The Thimble? The Boot? When a family opens a board game, a mom or dad may go for the rule book, but the kids always go for the game pieces. Their first concern: who do they "get to be?" Some players will spend hours tweaking their avatars, just as children spend lots of time arguing over which game token they'll use.

Kids love to pretend, to try on different roles, as they're still learning who they are. Grown-ups love to play games and pretend, too, to escape from whom they've become. And as players of all ages get more sophisticated, they're looking for more interesting roles to play.

Far Cry 3 lead writer Jeffrey Yohalem has suggested that game developers should treat their players like method actors. He said narrative designers must "understand a character's psychological motives, perform their actions, and connect their experiences with your own. The same can be said of a character and its player."[42]

Why should actors be the only lucky ones? Robert Downey Jr. gets to play Iron Man. In the *Iron Man* games, so can you!

AGENCY VS. EMOTIONAL ARC

So, how do you write a good PC that your players will bond with? First, you will need to determine with the gameplay designers how much

---

42 http://www.polygon.com/2013/3/31/4150956/far-cry-3-writer-method-acting-gdc-2013

"CHARACTER CREATION" IS NOT CREATING CHARACTERS

Writing a great character is different from the process of character (avatar) creation that is familiar to many video game players. In games like *World of Warcraft*, *Fallout 3*, and many others (including many sports games), players must click through a Character Creation module before beginning the gameplay. Here, players choose their avatar's attributes, such as their name, race, gender, build, facial features, hair style, clothing—the list can go on and on. Some of the *Saints Row* games even allow you to choose how your character sounds when speaking and moves when walking. But customizing your avatar is not the same as writing a character.

Yes, you can play Commander Shepherd as a woman or a man in *Mass Effect* (and this is awesome), but it does not directly impact the narrative of the story. Character creation does allow the player some agency in the "casting" of the protagonist. Players have posted detailed instructions on how to make an avatar in *Dragon Age: Inquisition* that looks like Daenerys Targaryen from *Game of Thrones*, bridging the realms of video games, cable TV, and the desire to create fan fiction. But that is not character creation; it is casting. The parts have already been written by the writers or the designers and—mirroring the same creative process of TV, movie, and play writing—the casting comes last.

——

agency the PC will have in the course of the game. Think of agency as the control that players feel they have in a game. How can the player affect their own course of actions and identity? In *Super Mario Bros.*, you played as Mario (no choices there) and could only travel left to right across the level (you could move right to left, but never reverse the level's rightward drift). You could choose to kill guys by (usually) jumping on top of them, or you could avoid them entirely. You were always Mario unless you powered up into a double-sized Mario or into a flame ball–shooting Mario. In some levels you could choose underground shortcuts rather than the main path through the level. But the vast majority of the time you were regular Mario, jumping on top of enemies. So you had limited agency of *action*, and almost no agency of *identity*.

In your game, will the player have almost total, *Skyrim*-like control over the PC's identity and actions, or will they play a mute, off-screen

PC, as in the *StarCraft* and *StarCraft 2* campaigns—a trusted, nameless ally who watches the drama of the story unfold between levels?

The latter case is easier to write, because you're essentially creating a non-interactive story. The PC is a passive observer of the action of the story, but an active driver of the gameplay. The PC does not emotionally change, although the characters around him do.

Video games should reach beyond this, when possible. In many games the only arc that occurs is an increase in ability—you may get new abilities (flight) as well as upgrades to existing abilities (your sword swings do double damage). The PC gains more tools, powers, and abilities as he or she progresses through the levels of the game. Even in mobile games, the PC can accumulate coins, special skills (*Temple Run*), or unlock levels (*Angry Birds, Candy Crush Saga*). These power-ups might be the only way for the PC to change.

Dynamic games should not just be about dynamic gameplay. They should feature characters that change and go on an emotional journey.

CHARACTERS IN CONFLICT MUST MAKE CHOICES

We watch movies, we read books, we binge on television shows to watch characters agonize over difficult choices. What will they do when they are betrayed? What is their reaction when lied to? What will happen when they find out the truth? What choices will they make? From comedy to drama—stories are all about characters making choices. (Comedy is often about watching the fallout from characters making the wrong choice.)

Choices sculpt character. A fireman drives home from work and saves a family from a burning house—not much of a choice. A bank robber driving home from a successful bank robbery sees the same house and chooses to save the family—that's a story. You have to make the choices difficult for the character or you don't have drama.

Gameplay—the action of the journey—provides the player with many choices. Dodge? Run? Gun? Knife? Grenade? Sneak past the bad guys? These are not dramatic choices. For a story to work, a character should be proactive, making a choice to go on a quest for a primal reason.

Why go slay the dragon if you don't have to go slay the dragon? Katniss Everdeen makes a choice in *The Hunger Games* to take the place of her sister Primrose. That choice leads to her to fight in the games and then lead a revolution. Michael Corleone makes a choice to protect his father, Vito, even though it means assuming his mantle in the family business. Notice how both choices involve family. As the Vault Dweller in *Fallout 3*, you learn your father has disappeared, and you choose to go into the post-Apocalyptic Capital Wasteland to find him. Again, family. In *Gone Home*, you explore the empty house in order to learn the fate of your family.

If you can reduce your game to a primal emotion, then the player can relate on a visceral level. Primal emotions are feelings we experience in our guts: the love of family, the longing for safety, the will to survive, the urge for revenge, the temptation to hate.

Stories and quests are stronger when characters are motivated by a primal emotion. *Motivation* is not just an actor's word. It needs to be the writer's word as well. Always ask yourself *why?* Why is my character behaving in this way? In *Dead Space*, Isaac's primal emotion is the will to survive. Survival horror is a genre that has always worked well in video games: *Resident Evil, Silent Hill, Dead Island*. They typically couple scary monsters with a general lack of agency. You have limited movement options, limited weapons, very little ammo. Like horror movie directors, horror game designers are very good at holding back information and options to keep you very afraid of what lies panting beyond the next door.

What about some other primal emotions? Where does love belong in a video game? Does it belong? We have seen Link's love in the *Legend of Zelda* games. We have seen it in the *Final Fantasy* games. In *Braid*, Tim is on a journey fueled by love. In *Nintendogs*, you love your digital puppies.

Kratos wants revenge—revenge is primal. Niko in *Grand Theft Auto IV* has come to America looking for his piece of the American dream, but also to escape the violence and poverty of his old country. He wants to survive and to thrive.

Audiences connect with what they understand on an emotional level. We are not saying this is the reason people want to play a game.

No. But primal emotions and backstory can be one of the many reasons that people love your game, and want to replay it, and tell their friends about it. It's a reason to care about what happens in the game.

A good story brings all these elements together. The father/son story at the heart of *Grand Theft Auto V* is not the reason we bought the game, but it's one of the reasons we became emotionally invested, and it provides an engaging story line. Your game story is working if players, rather than clicking through the cut scenes to get to the gameplay, sometimes find themselves rushing through the gameplay to learn *what happens next*? Ideally, you and your team are able to deliver story content during gameplay. *Grand Theft Auto V*, for example, does this with dialogue between characters as they ride in your car to the next mission.

Think of all this behind-the-scenes character work like writing code. If you are running an app or a program, you don't see the code. The engineers and programmers have. They spent many hours making the app work and fixing the bugs. The writer does the same for characters: decides on the inner conflict for your character that makes the quest of the game not just difficult for the player (action) but difficult for the character (emotion).

Joel in *The Last of Us* no longer wants to be a father. He feels he had that chance and lost it. When tasked with guiding Ellie, it is the last thing he wants to do and he fights it every step of the way, only to become a father again by the end of the game.

TO BE (PRESS A) OR NOT TO BE (PRESS B)

Game characters have more choices in stories than in any other medium. Can you imagine if during Hamlet's famous soliloquy, the Melancholy Dane waited for the audience to choose whether he should exist or not? Audiences are passive in every other form of narrative. (Works of "participatory theater" such as *Tony n' Tina's Wedding* being among the few exceptions.) But audiences generally cannot directly affect the story. It has been said that all movies are about *hope* and *fear*: You *hope* that characters make the right choice, you *fear* that they won't.

In traditional dramatic structure, the protagonist of the story makes a choice to go on the journey. This is usually at the end of the first act. In a television show it might be the end of the pilot episode that propels the series (*Lost:* How are we going to get off the island?), or in a movie or book when Harry gets to Hogwarts (*Harry Potter and The Sorcerer's Stone*). The first act choice gets the movie going. Every choice along the way pushes the story forward, revealing character and leading toward their emotional transformation.

Katniss makes a choice to take her sister's place in the Hunger Games. She then chooses not to impress the sponsors. She chooses not to kill the other tributes. She chooses Peta. She chooses to make two sequels.

A good story is crafted so that when the narrative kicks into gear, the player/protagonist has no choice but to go on the journey. Luke has to save the princess in *Star Wars*. Well, he doesn't *have* to. If he doesn't there is no movie and the Empire wins and he never gets off that planet. He has to do it. He "refuses the call" for a matter of seconds . . . just long enough to see the crispy bodies of his poor aunt and uncle. (Family again!) From that point forward, he's in it to win it. (Although he still says "I can't . . ." a lot.)

Dramatic choices in video game cinematics play out in this same fashion. The gameplay stops and the story kicks in. We continue to play so that the story can unfold.

CHOICES MUST LEAD TO CONSEQUENCES

Plays are unique because we see live emotion played out in front of our eyes. Actors on a stage. Really special. Movies are unique because of the close-up. The characters are sixty feet tall on a giant IMAX screen. We are transported around worlds. TV is unique because the story is brought into our home. We invite characters into our lives. We often prance naked and eat breakfast before them.

Games are unique because of the choices their players get to make. The platforms for delivery of content have stabilized (PCs, consoles, tablets, and phones), but what is constantly changing is their ability to carry and convey more information. That is, the computers have gotten smarter, and the chips can hold more data. This doesn't just mean better visuals; it means a better artificial intelligence (AI) system is built into a game. So when a player has a character make a choice in a game, the story has the potential to evolve.

We say *potential*, because we feel this is the direction games are going, although we're not quite there yet. For years growing up we had heard about hundreds of TV channels and video-on-demand for movies and television—and it's finally here. Bob and Keith both dreamed for years of having a library of every *Star Trek* episode that they could call up whenever they wanted to; they can both now die in peace. The promise of truly interactive narrative, where a player's choices can meaningfully impact a game's story and world, is getting closer and closer.

For years gamers were presented with choices that were not really choices. In *BioShock*, you can harvest a Little Sister for her Adam (something you need to survive and power up) OR you can choose to save that Little Sister. However, it turns out that at the end of the game, there is not much difference. If you save the Little Sister, there are other ways to obtain Adam and it doesn't affect the end-of-game cut scene much. (You do unlock an achievement, however).

Fallout 3 offered a glimpse into the future of gaming in the way you as the Vault Dweller choose to deal with Megaton. This was the town built around the unexploded nuclear bomb that you encounter after you leave Vault 101. As you explore the town, you quickly discover that if you follow a certain quest line, you have the choice either to disarm the bomb or to blow it up from a safe distance, thereby destroying the town. Blowing up the town led to one conclusion of the game, as did disarming the bomb. You can replay the game and make a different choice, and explore a different outcome and ending. The choice you make branches the narrative in a more significant way.

In *Fable 2,* if you were mean to villagers, then later in the story when you returned to that same town, the villagers would remember how you treated them and have the proper response based on the choice you made.

The *Mass Effect* trilogy keeps your choices logged over its last two parts, influencing the ending of each part and the conclusion of the saga. Choices you make influence your gameplay experience. Which one is the right choice? It is up to you to decide. There are thousands of different variations of the game. A *Mass Effect* movie has been in development in Hollywood for a long time. Why is the movie so hard to make? One of the first screenwriters on the project, Mark Protosevich (*Thor, I Am Legend*) said, "It was the first game adaptation I did and it will probably be the only one. They're hard. I will freely admit it was hard. Because—especially with *Mass Effect*—there's just so much material. Narratively, with the game, you're talking about nine, ten hours of narrative you're jamming into two hours."[43]

One of the surprise game hits of 2014 was *Middle-earth: Shadow of Mordor*, which features a "nemesis" system. The nemeses "are randomly named enemies in Sauron's Army that are generated uniquely with each playthrough of the game. Each nemesis has its own personality and will rise or fall within their social structure as the game progresses. They are affected by [the PC] Talion's actions, and each will react differently to Talion's incursion into Mordor, be it fight, flight, or some other reaction."[44] So your encounters with the enemy affect your character's choices and subsequent missions, which affect subsequent choices, and so on.

All this leads to the holy grail of game narrative when true choice leads to true consequence. *BioShock* creator Ken Levine is working on a new interactive story system. His goal is to create "narrative elements that are non-linear and interact with each other" and intends for "all narrative elements to trigger off player action."[45] Mr. Levine has called this "narrative Legos" and envisions a game where every choice influences and creates the narrative for the individual. He is aiming to push

43 http://badassdigest.com/2013/10/03/why-mass-effect-will-be-the-only-video-game-movie-mark-protosevitch-writes/

44 http://www.ign.com/wikis/middle-earth-shadow-of-mordor/The_Nemesis_System

45 http://gamerant.com/bioshock-ken-levine-finished-with-linear-narratives/

"the art of storytelling forward in video games."[46] Are we closer to a game that features non-linear narrative based completely on player choices but steeped in rich narrative structure?

It seems so.

But what happens when players have total autonomy? Even with a limited amount of choices in games now, players tend to make the "right" choice: the morally correct one. Telltale Games, developers of the *Walking Dead* games, were surprised to learn that when faced with a choice to do good or evil, players opted for good. According to their senior director of marketing, Richard Iggo:

> Some of the stats we've seen coming back from player decisions have created a perception that even in dire times—and when faced with no-win situations where each decision is morally grey—the majority of people will try to do the 'right' thing if they can, even if there's really no 'right' decision to be made. [. . .] It's fascinating because even when we offer players a decision where the apparently darker option might make sense from a purely logical point of view, they'll often try to choose the 'higher' ground at personal cost even if that means being put in danger or having a relationship with another character suffer because of it.[47]

46 http://www.polygon.com/2013/10/9/4816828/ken-levines-next-big-thing-isnt-so-much-a-game-as-it-is-a-reinvention

47 http://venturebeat.com/2012/08/15/telltale-games-the-walking-dead-statistics-trailer/

Speaking Through Your Characters

YOUR CHARACTERS should not sound alike. Ever. It is boring. Who wants to hear the same type of person keep speaking? We want characters who both act and sound different from each other. Kirk, Spock, and McCoy—all want the same thing but have different approaches and different means of communicating their emotions (even Spock). Han Solo and Luke Skywalker act and sound very different, even though they're on the same team.

Dialogue is the emotional DNA of all characters. It reveals who and what they might be.

1 **KRATOS, MARIO, AND NIKO BELLIC GET STUCK IN AN ELEVATOR . . .**
Using screenplay format, write a dialogue scene in which three of your favorite video game characters get stuck in an elevator. How do they react? What do they do? Kratos would want to hack and slash his way out. Niko would think he was being set up to be whacked. Mario might try to fix it, only to make it worse. We want you to write in different character voices. Minimize the character descriptions and action. Focus on their dialogue.

2 **FIND YOUR CHARACTER'S VOICE**
Let's focus on the voice of the main character of Your Game. In the first person, write a three-paragraph monologue in that main character's voice. They can talk about what is happening now in the story. They can talk about the past. They can talk about their expectations. It doesn't

matter. What does matter is that you begin to get a sense of who your main character is. What if you know your character is an elf enslaved by humans? What does he (or she) dream about? What keeps them going each day?

3 WRITE BARKS FOR YOUR CHARACTER

Based on what you've written about Your Game's PC in your Game Journal and in the previous exercise, write:

1. Eight different lines the PC would say as they are about to attack.
2. Eight different lines the PC would say as they are attacked.
3. Four different lines they would say if they were near death.
4. Four different lines they would say if they were near victory (over an opponent, not the entire game).
5. Eight different lines they would say if they were idle (prompting player input).

You should do this exercise in Excel or a similar spreadsheet program (since that's the way professional game writers would do it). Here's a sample format:

DIRECTION	LINE	TRIGGER
		Attacking
		Attacking
		Attacking
		Attacking
		Attacking
		Attacking
		Attacking

In this example "Direction" means the feeling the actor should convey in the line of dialogue (if it's not obvious from the line itself). For example, depending upon your PC's emotional makeup, they might be angry or excited as they attack, or they might in another instance be fearful. The Direction column helps save time during the recording session. (Most full video game scripts have other columns for comments, notes, sound file names, and so forth.)

CHAPTER 07

GAME DESIGN BASICS FOR WRITERS

IT'S ONLY A GAME—AND THAT'S A PRETTY GOOD THING

Plays have live performances. Actors take the stage and drama unfolds before our eyes. Movies make us believe in the unbelievable. They are a shared communal experience in cathedrals of imagination. A big popcorn movie on a summer Friday night transports the audience and sends spirits soaring (or cowering, if it's a horror film). Audiences become so involved that they tweet reactions to the movie as they're watching it.

Games takes this one step further and allow the viewer to participate in the action and, to a certain extent, set the pace of the action. The player controls the character and interacts with the game world. You see an object. Pick it up. Use it (or don't). You react. You make choices. You actively participate in the story. It's not a movie. It's not a play. It's a video game—and that's a pretty good thing.

If you made a "Christmas Tree of Player Expectations," it might look like this:

Participate

HERO

PLOT

GAMEPLAY

Notice that gameplay is the huge base. That's where the presents are. Without gameplay, there is no game. That's why the players are playing; if they wanted just a story, they're read a book or see a movie. The setting may be cool and the protagonist may be interesting, but without gameplay, you've got a webisode. Or worse.

Gameplay is what the players get to do in the game. This is where they get to Slay the Dragon. But how precisely will they do that? Do they have to find a magic arrow, build a catapult, swindle a peddler for an evil potion? Gameplay brings the players into the game and makes them active participants in the outcome of the story. We discussed this when we defined *mechanics* in Chapter 01. Game mechanics are the verbs at the player's disposal.

Gone Home designer Steve Gaynor writes this in the booklet that accompanies the game: "Video game writing does not happen in a vacuum. What's so exciting (and often challenging) about the process is that it's integrally intertwined with the design of the game itself."[48]

GAMEPLAY IS THE CORE BUILDING BLOCK OF INTERACTIVE NARRATIVE

This is not a book on game design. Having said that, let's talk about game design. Because no one can write for, create, develop, or produce a game without understanding the basics of creating gameplay.

Veteran game writer Haris Orkin (*Dead Island*, *Dying Light*) said that writing is

> a collaboration on movies and plays as well but even more so for games in a way, because the world is being built by other people . . . You have to work with game designers, level designers, the artists; it's really collaboration between all of it, because the story is told by every part of the game, as much by the level design and the art as it is by writing. The dialogue in a way is the least important part of telling a story; you don't really need that necessarily to tell a story in a game.[49]

[handwritten annotations: "most collab. art form", "dialogue < action"]

---

48 http://www.gonehomegame.com

49 http://kotaku.com/5988751/what-in-the-world-do-video-game-writers-do-the-minds-behind-some-of-last-years-biggest-games-explain

Writing is working on every aspect of the story. It's never just about the dialogue. Video game writers should be part of every development team. Games are one production where the project benefits from having the writer(s) "on the set" from day one. (This is a practice that film directors have not eagerly embraced.) The writer needs to know what the player is capable of doing in the game so they can work on making those mechanics emotionally resonant with the character in the story.

WHAT IS A GAME DESIGNER?

Let's discuss one of the most abused terms in the interactive field: "Game Designer." Our preferred term is "gameplay designer" because it's more precise. Gameplay designers design, and refine, and balance gameplay. That's true both on the engine level and on the level level (sorry, we had to).

What they don't do is create the game's look (that's the art director/visual designer), create the look of the environments or characters (that's the concept artist or character designer), program the game (that's the programmers), design the audio scheme (that's the sound designer), or "direct" the game. (Some do, but this role is typically filled by a lead game designer or a creative director.) They collaborate with all of the above, however.

What they do is, from paper prototype to final release, focus on whether the player is having fun. And making fun is hard work. Are the controls working? Is the player too powerful? Is the player not powerful enough? Does the player have a fair chance in the boss fight? Is this puzzle too obscure to be solved other than by random guessing? Does the level "flow"? Does the game "flow"? (Meaning, are there any lulls where a player is likely to get frustrated or lose interest?) They work side-by-side with (and sometimes double as) level designers, narrative designers, balance designers, user interface designers, and content designers. They communicate often with game testers and community managers to get gameplay feedback. They play their own game every day, but because this has its limits (you're only stumped by a puzzle once), they spend a good deal of time watching other people play their game. This gameplay testing process is iterative, in that they will get feedback, work with the rest of the team to absorb that feedback and tweak the gameplay, then test the tweaked version for further feedback. Lather. Rinse. Repeat.

Gameplay Balance and Narrative Balance

Frustration in gameplay should never impede the story. Ideally, the gameplay should always be challenging, but it should never make the player want to put down the game—or, worse, fling the controller at the TV. Conversely, a game must have strong challenges, otherwise it gets boring.

Gameplay balance optimizes challenge with difficulty. It's a goal designers are constantly working toward. Game writers deal with a very similar concept, and that's a *narrative balance*, which optimizes emotional involvement with interactivity. In other words, keeping the player involved in the story *while* they play the game—as opposed to merely between gameplay levels. Otherwise, they're just watching a movie in chunks.

Ask any gameplay designer how difficult it is to balance a game, and you'll get an earful. The concept of narrative balance is still relatively new and achieving it is just as challenging. It can be very frustrating. Like learning to walk, you're going to scrape your knees a lot as you discover how to navigate this new narrative playground.

OUR THEORY OF FUN

I hope we've established at this point that the essence of drama is conflict. What do you think is the essence of fun?

Take a minute to think about it. We'll wait. Pretend the *Final Jeopardy* jingle is playing.

The essence of fun is . . . surprise!

(Did that surprise you?)

Think about it. What was the first game you ever played? It wasn't a video game, or a board game, or even a playground game.

It was *peek-a-boo*. Which is less an actual game, really, than adults toying with the fact that babies' brains are still developing. Yet we squealed in delight when our grandma would pull her hands away and reveal her smiling face. "Surprise! There's grandma!"

So many game mechanics center around surprise: from turning over a card in

Solitaire to looting your bazillionth demon corpse in *Diablo*. Did you get what you were hoping for? Usually, no. *But sometimes you do!*

It is the challenge, the difficult-ness, the uncertainty of outcome, that makes gameplay *fun*. Think about it. Is turning on a light switch fun? No. We expect the light to go on every time. Is playing catch with your parents (or your children) fun? Absolutely. We're surprised and delighted when we (or they) succeed at catching the ball.

Speaking of balls, almost all sports are studies in uncertain, improbable success. We're surprised when baseball batters get a base hit. The game is rigged against them. (A "good" batter only gets on base once for every three or four at-bats.) We're surprised when the receiver catches the football (or the linebacker intercepts it). The ball is designed to be hard to catch, and there are eleven huge guys trying to stop that from happening. The late Robin Williams, himself an avid video game player, has a classic riff on the sadistic Scotsman who invented golf.[50] Talk about a game where success is elusive! Yet people have played golf for centuries, because they delight in the surprise of connecting a perfect stroke with the ball and sending it down the fairway toward the pin.

Gameplay designers love it when their players are feeling *fiero*, an Italian word loosely translated as "pride in overcoming adversity." Our feeling is that the root of *fiero* is surprise, because if you expected to overcome the obstacle, then it wasn't much of an obstacle in the first place, was it?

———

Does Gameplay Stop Narrative? Does the Story Stop the Gameplay?

The rule we try to follow is to ask ourselves, at any given moment in the game: "Are the emotions the player is likely feeling because of the *gameplay* enhanced by the *story*?"

During a period of furious action, like a firefight in a shooter, or a race in a driving game, the player's feelings of anger, fear, and suspense work with story beats that reflect those emotions.

Moments in which the player is searching for something, or exploring an unknown, lonely environment, work with story beats that might reflect loss, confusion, mourning, or mystery.

What if the player is exploring a beautiful environment? Story beats relating to love, satisfaction, triumph, promise, or joy might work well.

[handwritten margin note: emotions b/c gameplay enhanced by story?]

———

50 http://www.businessinsider.com/robin-williams-on-golf-2014-8

The point is not to grind the gears. Players will complain if you yank them from their player-feelings and push them into dissonant story-feelings. But if the story-feelings are in harmony with the player-feelings, the combined experience can be greater than the sum of the two parts (gameplay and story).

Gameplay Has to Be the Story of the Game

What the player does in the game must reflect the story and theme of the game. It should mesh with the narrative. Borrowing from other mediums, we think all mechanics should be considered as *active verbs*. Screenwriters, directors, and actors always (well, we hope) think in terms of active verbs. A good scene is constructed with this question in mind: *Who wants what in this scene?*

The late Mike Nichols' (*The Graduate, The Birdcage*) approach to writing and directing was that every scene should be a fight, a seduction, or a negotiation.[51] Game levels and movie scenes are very similar. In *Finding Nemo*, Marlin wants to escape Bruce the Shark. Marlin wants to live. Bruce the Shark wants to eat Marlin. (He fell off the "fish are friends, not food" wagon a few moments earlier.) Someone wins this scene (Marlin and Dory do, by escaping alive). In *BioShock*, at any given moment, Jack (you) is trying to survive and escape Rapture. You might have to take a picture of the Splicers to fulfill a mission. This requires you to fight off the Splicers (gameplay), find a camera (gameplay), and take a good photo (gameplay), all without being killed.

MECHANICS = ACTIVE VERBS

If the player is the protagonist of the game, you need to give the protagonist something to do in the scene. Writers give characters objectives when writing a scene. In the opening moments of *Guardians of the Galaxy*, Peter Quill (Starlord, man!) wants to steal an orb. When confronted by Korath, his objective is to escape. In *Inception*, Jack wants to "incept" an idea into someone's consciousness. How does he do this? Through a

---

51 http://www.slate.com/blogs/browbeat/2014/11/20/mike_nichols_dead_at_83_watch_three_of_his_best_scenes_from_the_movies_video.html

series of actions. The actions are translated in the story as verbs.

You should think about gameplay mechanics as active verbs. The gameplay designer has to develop a concept (active verb "to dance") into a system of algorithms that can be implemented through code (and art, and audio) so that the player can actually play a dance game.

That's why it's tricky.

But a game mechanic by itself is meaningless. It needs the *content*.

Mario jumping is just Mario jumping.

But when you put Mario in a *Super Mario Bros.* level, and give him bricks to smash and enemies to defeat, and allow him to use a jumping mechanic to explore the environment, it becomes fun.

The core mechanic of *Angry Birds* is basically shooting rubber bands. But the design of the pig forts—and the choices of which type of bird to shoot when—make up the content of this multi-billion-dollar franchise.

We prefer the word content because it's broader than "level design."

Content can refer to enemies, pick-ups, flavor text, dialogue, sound effects, props, etc. Anything meaningful to the player in the game environment (or in the menu space between real life and the game environment) is content.

This is different from assets, which refer to anything that can be seen or heard in the game. Assets are meaningful to the creators. Very often assets are content, but oftentimes there are assets in the game (animations, bump maps, collision maps) that are very important to the game's function, but which we the players never see.

If the mechanic is a hammer, the content is the nails.

Finally, we need a play goal. Rescue the princess. Slay the Dragon. Survive.

In the American board games that we grew up playing, the instructions always began with a big sentence in bold at the top of the first page (or inside the box lid): THE OBJECT OF THE GAME.

The object of most games is to "win" or to "beat the game." Most of us as players expect that there will be some sort of end to the game if we succeed at playing through the content.

Obviously, some games are unwinnable. If you think back to the quarter-eating games from the 1980s—*Space Invaders, Asteroids, Pac-Man*—the object of the game was to play as long as you could or, if you had mad skillz, to "make the board" by putting your initials onto the high score list that would display after the game ended. You counted that as a win.

Some games can be beaten, but they contain so much extra content or so many features that you can keep playing long after you're finished with the main story.

Just as game mechanics are player actions, the key to narrative design is coming up with a context for those player actions that make story sense, that happen in an intriguing world, and that make the player want to continue to explore the world through those mechanics.

How do you get the story into the game in an interesting and playable way? By providing *context for the gameplay*. For example, as you make your way through the levels of *BioShock*, you are often confronted by these annoying flying turrets that hover around, shooting at you. The only ways to beat them are either to destroy them (which is hard, and wastes precious ammo), or to deactivate them (which is still challenging, but less risky). If you choose to shut them off, you need to get to their control console and crack the code. Cracking the code is the gameplay. It's a puzzle. You have to solve the puzzle to survive. The gameplay exists within the story context. Otherwise, why would you bother with the puzzle?

MECHANICS & CONTEXT

Following is a chart that lists some example game mechanics, the story context built around that mechanic, and player emotions that should result. When all the gears mesh, you as the narrative designer are helping to create content that drives player emotion by making the game mechanics organic to the story.

GAME	MECHANIC	CONTEXT	FEELINGS
Grand Theft Auto	Racing	Escaping the police	Fear, suspense, *fiero*
Injustice	Fighting	Saving the world	Triumph, anger, excitement
Minecraft	Building	Sheltering from the Creepers	Satisfaction, relief, fear
Dead Space	Exploring	Escaping the haunted ship	Dread, anxiety, fear
FIFA	Running, kicking	Playing in the World Cup	Excitement, suspense, *fiero*
Call of Duty	Shooting	Squad-level urban combat	Camaraderie, fear, triumph
Any *Lego* game	Destroying, collecting, building	Heroic fantasy	Joy, wonder, competence, power
L.A. Noire	Investigating, interviewing	Detective work	Pensiveness, anomie

In filmmaking, we talk about whether a scene is "on the spine." Sometimes, scenes go off the rails in the rewriting, shooting, or editing process. The scene seems like a mere *activity* that does not lead to anything, or is not motivated. Ernest Hemingway never played a video game in his life, but he had sound advice for game developers: *never mistake motion for action.* Action has a reason to be there. Motion does not. It might be entertaining for a while, but you never want to take the viewer out of the story, or the player out of the game.

The action of the game has to mirror the emotion of the story. This is what leads to *empathetic immersion.* The player should ideally feel empathy—an emotional connection—to what's happening on the screen. This connection of emotion and action is what game creators should constantly be striving for, difficult though it may be. It's where the player and story become one; where the players are so absorbed in the game action they don't want to stop playing. They don't want to stop watching. They want to stay in the world because they feel they can help to decide the outcome. And that is something only games can do.

Playing with Gameplay

1 DESCRIBE TEN MINUTES OF GAMEPLAY

Play a game. In your Game Journal, describe the first (or any) ten minutes of gameplay. You should have complete control of your character and not be stuck in any noninteractive story sequences. Describe in your Game Journal what you were doing, thinking, and feeling during those ten minutes. What did you get to do? How much freedom of action did you have?

2 ADD A MECHANIC TO YOUR FAVORITE GAME

Imagine (or replay some of) your favorite game. Now think of a game mechanic you might add that is not organic to that game. How would it change the game? How would you use it? For instance, what if you could *move* your plants in *Plants vs. Zombies*? How would that affect the player's experience? Would it make the game easier or harder?

3 CREATE A STORY BASED ON GAME MECHANICS

Remember that we've defined game mechanics as the *verbs*; those actions the player can take in the game. Here's a far-from-exhaustive list of twenty-five game mechanics.

1.	Accelerating and Decelerating	13.	Herding
2.	Arranging	14.	Jumping
3.	Attacking and Defending	15.	Matching
4.	Building	16.	Nurturing
5.	Buying and Selling	17.	Placing
6.	Catching	18.	Powering
7.	Conquering	19.	Seeking Information
8.	Contracting (with another player or an NPC)	20.	Selecting
9.	Directing	21.	Sequencing
10.	Discarding	22.	Shooting
11.	Enveloping	23.	Speaking
12.	Exchanging	24.	Taking
		25.	Voting

Get some dice to roll or coins to flip. Choose five mechanics at random from this list. (If you don't have dice or coins, try the free random number generator at www.random.org.)

Of those five random mechanics choose three and develop a one- or two-paragraph game pitch that uses the three mechanics. Describe the world where the game takes place, the PC, the goal, the antagonist(s), and how the three mechanics are used in the game world.

CHAPTER 08

THE HERO OF A THOUSAND LEVELS

QUESTS, LEVELS, AND MISSIONS: DISSECTING YOUR GAME

Although it's not a perfect comparison, scenes are to a movie what chapters are to a book and what levels are to a game. They're the chunks of content through which we consume the entire experience.

Not every game features discrete levels, and not every game that has discrete levels calls them that. They may be waves, boards, missions, quests, rounds, or stages. A game may borrow the nomenclature of passive media and call its levels scenes, chapters, books, or passages. Some games allow you to multitask, making progress on and switching between multiple missions at once. *World of Warcraft* allows you to work on up to twenty-five quests at once; it's a vast playground for the focus-impaired.

But whatever you call the component parts of your game, let's for simplicity's sake refer to them here as levels.

As game players, we instinctually sense that each level should bring us some *gameplay progress*. Expanding our journey of action. Our expectation is that not only should completing a level bring us one step closer to beating the game, it should also enhance us in some way. We should learn a new ability, strengthen an existing ability, get a cool piece of gear, learn a secret about the world, or, at least, hone our skill, so that we'll enter the next level feeling more competent (and confident) at racing, jumping, puzzle solving, shooting, negotiating . . . whatever the core mechanic may be. If we're not rewarded with some type of gameplay progress, we risk feeling like the gameplay is just busywork.

reward = necessary work

Narrative progress

We have a similar expectation as an audience that each scene or episode should bring us some *narrative progress*—deepening our journey of emotion. Our hero gets a little wiser, the stakes get a little higher, the villain gets a little scarier. If the story isn't progressing in some manner, keeping us wondering what happens next, then we accuse it of being "episodic," which in this context is a bad word in Hollywood. (See synonyms at "meandering," or "time wasting.")

And yet, many game stories fall into this trap. We were very excited years ago when *Puzzle Quest* promised to be a puzzle game with an engaging story. The promise was that the story would motivate sessions of *Bejeweled*-like match-three gameplay, but sadly, though we're fond of the game, this proved not to be the case. Set in a familiar-seeming world of medieval fantasy, the lack of compelling characters and the endless subplot after subplot soon left us, sadly, clicking through the dialogue bubbles as fast as we could to get to the next puzzle. (We're bigger fans of *Marvel Puzzle Quest*, which makes good use of the Marvel Comics characters and features funny smack talk between the heroes and villains during the story bits. Plus, Squirrel Girl!)

As game writers, we should be learning from the best of today's golden age of television. *Breaking Bad*, *Mad Men*, *The Good Wife*, *Battlestar Galactica*, *The Wire*, *The Walking Dead*, and so many more we could list (*The Americans!*) have gotten so good at keeping us watching via plants and payoffs, complex anti-heroic characters, and lots of foreshadowing.

You need to know what the dramatic spine of the game is, the arc of each major character, how their goals could conflict, who could betray or abandon whom, and then lay the story out, piece by piece, level by level. If you walked into the writers' room of a television show, you would see a giant whiteboard that lays out the scenes of an episode, or even the episodes of a season. Game developers have similar level charts (often hanging in the hallway near the producer's or lead designer's office). These tend to break down to a fine detail what's happening with the gameplay in each level. However, games are becoming more story driven. Sam Lake, writer/producer at Remedy Entertainment, says, "... with the

Max Payne games, it was very important to have different levels in the story, both the external action and the internal struggles of the main character."[52]

We approach level design from a narrative design approach. Let's figure out what drives the story forward and then figure out what goes on inside the levels. Much like a character, we work with the external and the internal. What is the level? And then what happens inside the level?

LEVEL DESIGN IS STORY DESIGN

Levels are like chapters in a book, episodes in a television show, or scenes in a movie. Playing through the levels pushes the player through the narrative structure of the game. Here is our definition of a level:

> A level is a contained environment where the player/protagonist must achieve a goal, or a series of goals, in order to continue with the story or game and advance to the next level.

Inside the level there might be side quests or smaller goals that build to the larger goal of the level, and these might double as checkpoints: places where the game saves your progress and where you can return after your character dies. Levels vary in length. Some might take but a few minutes to play, while some might keep you sweating it out for an hour or more.

The Narrative Function of Levels

Levels are the chapters of your story. You should start small and go big and go bigger and then go bigger. The drama has to ramp up along with the gameplay. How does your hero grow in each level? What's your hero's goal in each level? Like the player, your hero has a goal for the entire game (Slaying the Dragon), but there needs to be a meaningful and recognizable and discreet goal for each level. Otherwise, it's just

---

52   http://www.theguardian.com/technology/gamesblog/2010/apr/30/alan-wake-remedy-sam-lake

another and another and another. Activity without purpose. Sound and fury, signifying nothing.

Levels, quests, and missions should all be fractal—self-similar—in structure. Your main story has a beginning, middle, and an end, *and so should each level, quest, and mission.*) all have BME

Once you define a goal for a level (know thy ending!) you should extrapolate its three-act structure: The Goal, the Complication, and the Resolution. Or the Thesis, the Antithesis, and the Synthesis. Or, from a punctuation standpoint:

? ! and .

? ! . .

The ? of the level is always, what does the PC want?

The ! is all the obstacles that stand in the way of that goal.

The . is the resolution. Did the PC reach the goal? If not, what stopped him? How does he react?

A Clue from Cartman's Creators

Trey Parker and Matt Stone built the profane monster that is *South Park* and conquered Broadway with *The Book of Mormon*. (They are also avid gamers, and once teamed up with Blizzard to produce a classic *WoW*-themed *South Park* episode.) A few years back they visited an NYU storytelling class and shared their secret to scene progression, and it's just as valuable to level progression. Their secret?

Two words: *therefore* and *but*. (With one "t." Let's make that clear. These are the *South Park* guys we're talking about, after all.)

The connection between one level and another should never be "and." Use instead "therefore," and "but." Because Level A, therefore Level B. Or, Level A, but (surprise!) Level B. "Therefore" suggests that finishing the level will have unintended consequences. "But" suggests that the next level begins with new information that will create further complications. Plans will go awry. We will have to adapt our strategy. *What will happen next?*

Stories and levels always need turning points to keep moving forward and using the words *therefore* and *but* are going to save you. *And*, on the other hand, will bury you. How many games have you played where the level objectives read like:

1. Go get the gnarled old walking stick, AND
2. Go get the dusty jewel, AND
3. Go find the rusty headpiece, AND
4. Take them all to the wizened wizard to reassemble into the Furious Staff of Rudeness, AND
5. Schlep the staff to the Ancient Split-Level Ranch-Style Temple in a Bad School District, AND
6. Use it to defeat the Undercaffeinated Temple Guardian, AND
7. Finally you get to enter the first dungeon . . .

It gets kind of boring kind of quickly, no matter how fun the gameplay is. *God of War* suffered from this a little bit. It seemed to take *forever* to plow through all the Cosmic Errands you had to run in order to get to Pandora's Box and finally face Ares. Why did we find it dull? Because the vast majority of its levels feature Kratos plowing through hundreds of mute monsters. This was exciting for the first big chunk of the game, but then it grew very tiresome. For so many levels, there were no sentient, speaking adversaries for him. The most dramatic conflict is *characters* in opposition. Monsters can be cool looking and scary and deadly and all, but they're basically animals.

Conversely, one of the reasons we feel the original *Metal Gear Solid* holds up so well after almost 20 years is that each level boss was a distinct and interesting *character*. Revolver Ocelot, Psycho Mantis, Sniper Wolf, Vulcan Raven . . . these weren't just passable heavy metal band names, they were distinct personalities (and sets of abilities) that challenged the PC, Solid Snake, on both a gameplay and an emotional level.

We don't mean to assert that man vs. monster, man vs. beast, or man vs. nature aren't great conflicts. They certainly can be. But those are *easy* to do with video games. Creating actual characters is a challenge (hopefully less so after you've read Chapter 05). But it's worthwhile. Human vs. Human (or human-acting alien) is inherently more engaging, more dramatic, than Mario jumping on mute Goombas.

We tend to cut a lot of dramatic corners when we develop games. We miss a lot of opportunities. Once we assign some AI to an enemy type, make sure it looks good, sounds good, and animates well, we think the job is done. What we don't do is think, who's sending these guys out? What's their beef with the PC? How do all these minions feel about being cannon fodder?

Think of the levels as *conceptual blocks* that move the story forward. Map out the journey as you would a trip, not just in terms of environments (the snow level, the sky level, the desert level, . . .) and enemies (yeti, rocs, sandworms, . . .), but looking ahead to whom our hero(es) will encounter, why, and how it will affect them—in terms of emotions as well as gameplay.

Card It Out

Index Cards

Writers have always used index cards—and will continue to do so—to craft their stories. (Lately, they may be using virtual index cards in writing software, but they're still using cards.) We recommend physical cards. Jot notions down on each one. Ideas for scenes. For arguments. For jokes. For characters. For settings. Each scene or *level* can be a card and you can move them around in any order you like. You might have different colors for different aspects of the scene (gameplay, character, environment, etc.), in which case each level would be a stack of each color. If you're missing a color, you're not done thinking about the level. Be sure to keep your Pyra-Grid handy.

Build your story through *narrative level design*. You can fill in the blanks as you go along and build the world along with the level designers, who will do the floor plans, enemy and pickup placement, and so forth.

Game writing, like most writing, is elliptical. You don't really start at the beginning and write through the end. You are figuring out and breaking the story in a continuous back and forth motion. *BME*

Structurally, each level has a beginning, a middle, and an end which drives us to the next level. The end of each level should be a *turning point* in the story that brings the narrative to the next part of the story. It needs to build. Remember Matt and Trey: *therefore* or *but*. *therefore but*

There are various ways to convey story content that set up the ministory of the level. We'll discuss some of these in the next chapter. It's all about context.

Don't think about player activity; think about the *events* that impact the story.

STORY BEATS BY LEVEL:
AN ANALYSIS OF *THE LAST OF US*

Begin to analyze games from a standpoint of levels, and what their function is in the greater story of the game. Let's look at *The Last of Us* and see how the story beats are stitched into the game's rather large, lengthy "chapters."

The Last of Us, written by Neil Druckmann. (The act designations are our own.)

ACT ONE

LEVEL: PROLOGUE

1. Joel and Sarah celebrate birthday. She gives Dad a broken watch.
2. Later that night, Joel shoots an infected intruder.
3. Joel, Sarah, and Tommy (Joel's brother) get to a car to escape.
4. During escape, the car crashes. They are trapped.
5. They are separated from Tommy.
6. The Army shoots Sarah in front of Joel.
7. Over the opening credits, we see the disease spreading, the world falling apart, and the rise of the Fireflies.

LEVEL: THE QUARANTINE ZONE

1. Twenty years later, Joel is a survivor. He is with Tess. Looking for weapons, looking for an arms dealer.
2. They learn from Marlene that Robert sold the guns to the Fireflies.
3. Marlene says they can earn the guns back if Joel agrees to do something.
4. Joel reluctantly agrees to smuggle Ellie out of the city.

ACT TWO

LEVEL: THE OUTSKIRTS

1. Joel the reluctant father has to take care of Ellie.
2. As they venture out of town, they are confronted by a patrol.
3. Ellie stabs a soldier. Joel kills the soldiers.
4. Joel learns that Ellie is *immune* and she might be the key to the cure.

LEVEL: DOWNTOWN

1. As the gameplay progresses, Joel is antagonistic toward Ellie.
2. He begins to lose his focus, as he slowly feels like a father again.
3. The goal is to get Ellie to Tommy and the Fireflies.
4. Joel makes the rules, acting more parental.

LEVEL: BILL'S TOWN

1. They seek a car from Bill, an old friend.
2. They have to get the parts to use the car.
3. They fight off "Clickers."
4. Ellie drives the car. Parent moment as they escape.

LEVELS: PITTSBURGH/THE SUBURBS

1. On the drive toward Pittsburgh, Joel and Ellie have father/daughter bonding moments.
2. We are at the *midpoint* and Joel is changing. He is no longer the hard-ass guy. He is becoming a parent again.
3. They encounter roadblocks, danger.
4. Ellie saves Joel.
5. The theme of endure and survive emerges as Ellie kills a man.
6. Joel teaches Ellie to use the gun.

LEVEL: TOMMY'S DAM

1. Joel and Ellie team up with Henry and Sam, two brothers.
2. Henry commits suicide after having to kill his infected brother.

LEVEL: THE UNIVERSITY

1. Joel and Ellie find Tommy.
2. Joel finds the Fireflies hospital.
3. Joel is attacked by bandits. Separated from Ellie. Joel is wounded.

LEVEL: LAKESIDE RESORT

1. Joel and Ellie hide out in the mountains.
2. Joel is on the brink of death.
3. Ellie goes to find food for him but is captured.
4. Ellie kills her captors as Joel finds her and consoles her.

LEVEL: BUS DEPOT

1. In the spring, Joel and Ellie arrive in Salt Lake City.
2. Captured by a Firefly patrol.

LEVEL: THE FIREFLY LAB

1. Marlene tells Joel that the Fireflies are going to operate on Ellie.
2. She will not survive the surgery but she might be the cure.
3. Joel kills the Fireflies and stops the operation.
4. He kills Marlene and escapes with the unconscious Ellie.

LEVEL: JACKSON

1. Ellie asks Joel what happened.
2. Joel lies – said the Fireflies were unable to find a cure.
3. Ellie asks Joel if his story is true.
4. Joel lies. Says it is.
5. Joel is the parent who doesn't want his child to die.

[handwritten margin notes: easily summarized actions / journey of action]

—

WHAT MUST HAPPEN IN YOUR LEVEL?

The external story beats of each level make up the *journey of emotion*. This is how we tell the story of the game that leads us to the character growth and change. What happens within the levels is the *journey of action*. This is the gameplay within the level that the player has to engage with and progress through in order to move on.

In a sense, all storytelling is problem solving. Scenes in movies and television have protagonists confronted with a series of problems they need to solve. In *Inception*, the problems that Cobb (Leonardo DiCaprio) and his team face are different, but connected on each "level" in the last act. In *The Dark Knight Rises*, Bruce Wayne faces many problems: defeat from Bane, having his back broken, being trapped in an ancient prison. He has to "solve" that problem and move on to the next phase of the story. In *Gravity*, Dr. Ryan "I hate space" Stone (Sandra Bullock) has to solve a series of problems which seem insurmountable in order to return safely to Earth. Each of the sequences or set pieces in these movies reminds us of video game levels. There's action, sure, but what makes the action dramatic are the stakes ~~involved and~~ the emotions at play in the characters we are rooting for.

Ideally, video game levels should work the same way. Sometimes they do; often they don't.

Here is what we feel levels should do:

Levels Need to Move the Story Forward
Q's answered + raised nor expand

With each level, the narrative should expand. Questions should be answered, but new questions should be raised. Jack in *BioShock* has to survive the deathtraps of each level in order to progress toward his goal: escaping Rapture. But each level teaches him (and us) a little more about his tormentor, Andrew Ryan, about the madhouse that is Rapture, and about himself.

Levels Should Have Clear Objectives
The main plot has the main goal of the story: the Dragon that must be Slayed. Each level has a goal as well. They can change mid-level (surprise is good!), as long as that change in goal is motivated by narrative complications. The PC's purpose needs to be grounded in the world of the story and flow organically from the story. *external + internal objective*

Ideally, you have both an external objective (cross the Chasm of Unsafe Lava) and an internal objective. The internal objective can be emotional (overcome your fear of fire; test the loyalty of the party member you suspect will betray you) or related to character abilities (learn how to jump higher, learn how to defeat a heretofore-unbeatable enemy type).

Levels Can Have Multiple or Mini Goals
Levels can be divided up with mini-goals, giving the player a series of missions, or campaigns within the game. As you want to raise the dramatic tension, the rising action level goals should start small and go big. If there are three mini-goals within the level, each one should become more difficult to achieve. But they should have some narrative distinction;

make some sort of story sense. *Doom* and its progeny spawned hundreds of maze-like game levels where your character had to find a red keycard, then a blue keycard, then place both keycards in the slot to open the door to the level boss. We can do better. We can make things more interesting and involving.

Levels Should Have Bosses   *Boss*

The "boss" is the final obstacle blocking the player-protagonist from advancing in the game. The boss is the biggest challenge on the level. A level boss is often a major NPC in the game (like Revolver Ocelot, et al., in *Metal Gear Solid*), but a boss can also be a unique puzzle or environmental challenge (disarm a bomb before the time runs out, solve the sphinx's riddle in three guesses).

Levels Should Start with a Punch and End with a Flurry

Players should be able to get into the action of the gameplay as soon as possible. If a noninteractive cinematic or other narrative tool is used to introduce the goal of the level, the game is more engaging if the gameplay begins right after that. The PC should not get an assignment and then wander around waiting for something to happen. Subsequent levels should end with the most exciting gameplay, and as soon as the goal is achieved, the level should end.

action ASAP

Levels Should Increase Agency

Levels need to increase agency so the player has a reason for playing. These can include the acquisitions of better weapons, skills, clothing, knowledge, etc. It could be an increase in abilities. Without the increase in agency it should be harder, but not impossible, to beat the game. The ability arc of the player needs to increase in relationship to how far into the game the player has played.

increase

There can be exceptions to this. One of our favorite twists in the original *Half-Life* is when the PC, Gordon Freeman, is captured, stripped of all his weapons, and left for dead in a trash compactor. It feels like a huge step backward in gameplay, and you as Freeman have to learn how *added difficulty*

to make do without the useful personal arsenal you'd been relying on to plow through waves of enemies. It's a great surprise and a great conceit around which to build a level—and it's completely organic to the story. *Of course* the bad guys would take his weapons when they captured Freeman.

Levels Should Provide Character Insight *character feeling*

Levels should provide information to the audience about what the character is feeling during the level. Levels can reveal character in such a way that deepens our understanding of and identification with the protagonists and the world around them. The giraffe moment in *The Last of Us* stands out to us as the writers break up the action with a very human moment. Parents take their children to the zoo. Here in the middle of this fractured father-daughter tale, Joel and Ellie pet a giraffe. It has nothing to do with gameplay but everything to do with story.

Levels Should Have Turning Points *dramatic tables turns*

Levels should have dramatic turning points; when expectations are met, things get boring. There is nothing wrong with setting up a false goal for the character and then turning the tables on the player. One of the first missions in *BioShock* is to get to a submarine to escape. What happens? The sub explodes!

Levels Should Foreshadow *foreshadow + integrate next level hint*

And then finally, is there any foreshadowing? Is there anything that draws the player into the next level other than, "You're awesome. You beat this level!" How about more challenges, right? Or any way of integrating the next level into the level you're playing. Can you drop a hint of what's to come, both story- and gameplay-wise?

And, finally . . .

Levels Should Be Fun

Otherwise, what's the point?

FIT YOUR IDEA IN THE GAME ENGINE

Game writers, both actual and aspiring, should play lots of games. You should always be playing, and keeping a careful eye on how the story unfolds and the world is revealed. You should develop "engine eye" in order to get an intuitive sense of what storytelling possibilities a particular game engine might support, and what's not possible or feasible.

Imagine if you were writing an episode of a traditional TV sitcom filmed with three cameras on a set on a soundstage, like *The Big Bang Theory* or *Two Broke Girls*. You would not suggest that the character open the living room door to a portal to another world where a fiery dragon lives, nor would you write an episode that takes the cast road tripping through the Italian Alps. You are confined by the limitations of the show's budget and the size of its actual soundstage.

Game engines—and levels created for those game engines—have similar boundaries, and the savvy writer or designer weaves these limitations into the story. In *Assassin's Creed*, if you reach the outer boundary of a level, a sparkling blue translucent wall keeps you from advancing. You are told this is because those memories have not yet been unlocked. One of the best ways for you to develop a sense of design is to use in-game level editors to create your own content. Some level editors even contain scripting functions that allow you to create story content alongside the gameplay. The *Little Big Planet* series can be considered a level editor that thinks it's a game. It allows you to put together a playable platform-jumping level in just a few minutes. (Most level editors are not supported by the developers that release them, however, and documentation is frequently lacking. Search the Web for fan-made tutorials and discussion threads if you need help.).

LEVEL DESIGN IMPACTS TRADITIONAL MEDIA

The two most successful recent "video game" movies aren't based on actual games, but they mimic their structure. Both *Snowpiercer* and *Edge of Tomorrow* feel like video games, in a good way. Each uses a level-by-level structure, with the protagonists unable to advance along their path until they solve knotty problems. *Snowpiercer* follows a group of rebels from the caboose of a post-apocalyptic train as they make their way to the engine. Each set of cars is more deadly—and dramatic— than the next. *Edge of Tomorrow* finds its hero (Tom Cruise) stuck in a *Groundhog Day*-like time loop. He has to die—and re-spawn—again and again in order to make baby steps toward his goal of saving Earth and escaping the time loop. It's the closest thing we have to *Dark Souls: The Movie* until we actually get *Dark Souls: The Movie*.

We have said that movies are not video games and video games are not movies—but the majority of the audience consuming content in the world today grew up with games. Just as game creators for years have been borrowing technique from cinema, game-savvy filmmakers are using interactive storytelling methods to create compelling new motion pictures.

DRAGON EXERCISES 08

Leveling Up

1 ANALYZE A LEVEL

A great way to learn anything is to reverse engineer it. Take it apart. We want you to reverse engineer a game level. Take a game you love and play it on a skill level that allows you to get through it quickly.

Choose a favorite level and map it out in your Game Journal. What happens on the level? Is there a beginning, middle, and end? How is the PC changed by playing the level? What was the PC's goal in the level? Did she succeed or fail?

2 WRITE A LEVEL-BY-LEVEL OUTLINE FOR YOUR GAME

You're far enough along to put what you've learned together to take Your Game to the next . . . level.

Begin to flesh out Your Game by outlining the story and character(s). Begin with a good title for Your Game and then write:

1. A two-or three-paragraph summary of the plot.
2. The cast of characters (the PC and the adversary, at minimum). Give a two- or three-sentence description of each character.
3. In three or four sentences per level (or quest, or mission), briefly describe each level from both a story and gameplay standpoint.
4. Summarize the gameplay in Your Game. Describe the core game mechanics. How do these integrate into your story? How does gameplay evolve as the game progresses?

CHAPTER 09

BUILDING YOUR WORLD WITH THE NARRATIVE DESIGN TOOLBOX

SCREENWRITERS FOLLOW A somewhat clear linear path toward getting their work produced. The writer of the original screenplay sells it to the marketplace, or is hired to write on assignment for a studio. A screenwriter who is good with dialogue might be brought in to punch up the dialogue; an action writer might be brought in to write action; a joke writer can come in and sharpen the comedy. The original writer might stay on, but they usually do not. But so many movies that we hold as modern iconic cinema: *Pulp Fiction, The Usual Suspects, Boogie Nights, There Will Be Blood* . . . all were writer-driven. The screenwriter developed the idea, wrote it, and then put it on the market to get it made.

The television writer might pitch an idea, sell it to a network, and then if it gets picked up will hire a writing staff where every person contributes to the writing of that show. A TV writer might be the showrunner (head producer) or one of several staff writers, or even a freelancer. There are a very finite number of ways writers define their roles in the world of film and television.

The writer of a CGI animated movie (*Wreck-It Ralph, Despicable Me,* the *Ice Age* franchise, any Pixar production), has the most in common with the world of writing for video games. Both require multidisciplinary teams that use complex technology which is constantly being upgraded and adapted over the course of the project. The truism with both CGI animation production and video games is that you're "still building the airplane while it's in flight."

It is a world where the writer works in collaboration from the beginning of the project but under the guidance of a creative producer, or a team of producers. The writer might then write the full script or scenes and the animation team might produce "animatics" to see whether a scene works or not.

Animated movies are *not* written by writers in the hope of selling them as movies. Writers do not pitch animated movies (unless it's based on pre-existing property, like Cressida Cowell's *How to Train Your Dragon* books). Animated movies, like video games, are developed in-house, sometimes hiring a writer to come work for the company for an extended period of time as the movie evolves.

As interactive narrative evolves, the role of the game writer also evolves. Forgetting any and all titles here (creative director, lead writer, narrative or content designer—they will vary from team to team) we want to focus in this chapter on what the writer of a video game might actually *do,* and discuss what tools are available for the writer to do her job concentrating on the process as it mirrors game development.

Games are not written. Games are developed. Games are built. Games are collaborative.

A writer auditioning for work at a video game company might be asked to submit samples. Jill Murray, a novelist turned WGA-nominated game writer for *Assassin's Creed: Liberation*, wrote young adult novels. Other writers come from film backgrounds, but most video game writers have always worked in video games and worked their way to their current position on "pen on paper" power.

Regardless of your writing background, before you can jump in and begin writing, here are some things you will need to know.

THE GAME CONCEPT DOCUMENT

Video games tend to be developed in house like animated movies. The creative director might work in concert with a lead writer to develop a *game concept document* (GCD). This might be a pitch document for the publisher, but it also serves the rest of the growing team that is building

GCD
Show themes, characters, + layout

the game. It is the concept "bible" for the adventure. In television circles, the bible is the document that describes the show, the themes, the characters, and lays out where the stories will flow from season one, and possibly more. Ron Moore's bible for *Battlestar Galactica* contains mission statements, detailed histories of the world, and everything else one can imagine. After reading his bible, you cannot help but be impressed by the level of detail to which Moore envisioned his series.

In Ken Levine's written pitch for *BioShock*, the game is called a "first person action horror."[53] It continues, "*BioShock* is a modern day nightmare of the terrifying nexus of religious fanaticism and unbounded science." If you read through the document, you might not recognize any of the names—but you will recognize the tone and the spirit of the game. That is the main purpose of the game concept document. Your GCD contains:

> The things you need to know about the game in order to write for the game that may or may not be in the game design document you may or may not help to write.

We'll discuss how you can put together your own GCD in the exercise following Chapter 12.

THE GAMEFLY PITCH

summarize in a few short sentences

You should be able to summarize your game in a few short sentences. We call this the GameFly pitch, because we like the GameFly rent-games-by-mail service, but you could also call it the "back of the box" pitch (or the "Steam" pitch, or the "Amazon" pitch . . .). Let's say you are looking to play a new game that you have never heard of. This is what you are doing when creating a game—you are building a world that no one has ever heard of or seen except you and your team. How do you describe it? Well, imagine it on the GameFly site:

---

53 http://irrationalgames.com/insider/from-the-vault-may/

> *The Order: 1886* is an ambitious action-adventure game set in a
> fictional version of London. Instead of charming ladies and Victorian
> blokes, *The Order*'s London is rife with terrifying monsters. In fact,
> all of human history has revolved around a war between men and
> this army of half-human abominations. You play as Galahad, a
> member of an ancient order of knights founded by King Arthur—you
> are sworn and duty-bound to protect the people of London. Luckily,
> your fellow knights are there to help you out, and you'll also have a
> ton of awesome steampunk-style technology on hand too. You'll fly
> zeppelins, use wireless communications, and fire an arsenal of exotic
> weapons at your monstrous foes.[54]

A couple of key phrases here to look for and to include when developing the pitch: there is a title and then there is the genre. Remember that the type of gameplay (platformer, brawler, RPG, et al) determines genres in games. In this case, "action-adventure" is a broad category, but one that promises multiple mechanics, not just shooting or just platform jumping.

There is also story. An overview. There is the *promise of the premise.* You know the world and what you will do. The phrase "you play as" is very important to the game pitch, as you are telling the player who the main character is.

"But my game is an indie!" you protest. All good. Indie games need awesome descriptions, as they don't have the luxury of TV spots and lots of media coverage to get their message out. Here is how *The Talos Principle* is summarized on Steam:

> *The Talos Principle* is a first-person puzzle game in the tradition
> of philosophical science fiction, made by Croteam, the creators of
> *Serious Sam*, and written by Tom Jubert (*FTL, The Swapper*) and
> Jonas Kyratzes (*The Sea Will Claim Everything*). As if awakening from
> a deep sleep, you find yourself in a strange, contradictory world of

---

54 http://www.gamefly.com/#!/game/The-Order-1886/5006497

ancient ruins and advanced technology. Tasked by your creator with solving a series of increasingly complex puzzles, you must decide whether to have faith or to ask the difficult questions: Who are you? What is your purpose? And what are you going to do about it?[55]

(We love that the writers get credit and recognition!) *read descriptions*

If you really want to sharpen your skills, start reading (and writing) the one- or two-sentence descriptions for mobile games on the App Store and Google Play. It's a merchandising nightmare. You generally have a small square image and *one or two sentences* (plus a good title) to grab the eye of browsers and get your game noticed.

Gameplay + story + you are the three must-have ingredients for the short game pitch.

But remember that you're building a world that players should want to play in.

IMAGINE YOUR WORLD—NOT SOMEONE ELSE'S

Writing great video games is the craft of building awesome worlds. The look of the game (its art direction—not just its graphics-rendering technology) plays such an important part of the immersive experience. It's not just eye candy like when you see a trailer for the fifteenth sequel to *The Hobbit*. This is eye candy that the player/viewer is going to explore; become a part of. But eye candy begins to look the same after a while. We like eye candy; but we like cool ideas even more.

At the risk of pissing off many developers, and friends, and fans, we feel it's time somebody stood up and made the following assertion:

Too many games look like too many other games!

We're not just talking art direction, here. We're talking play style, game design, and—mostly—world design. For decades, developers have fallen in love with a world they read about in a book (by J. R. R. Tolkien)

---

55 http://store.steampowered.com/app/257510/

create your own

or saw in a movie (by George Lucas) or played in a game (by yet another developer who was inspired by *Lord of the Rings* or *Star Wars*). Creatively, this has been like a snake eating its tail. It has *got* to stop if we are to mature as a medium. (And it is . . . more on this later.)

You're holding this book because you know that inside you there is a writer. Because you want to express yourself.

Awesome. Express *your* self. Show us the world inside *your* head.

You don't need to express Tolkien or Lucas or Stan Lee (sorry, Stan). They don't need your help.

At every turn, you should be asking yourself why you want to bring players into your world. What do you want to show them that you feel they should see? Granted, George R. R. Martin's *A Song of Ice and Fire* bears a passing resemblance to Middle Earth, but Martin's world is less about magic (dragons notwithstanding) and is much more about political drama. Martin's characters are at once more rapacious and more human. Ask yourself, do you want to reflect our world as you think it is, or as you wish it would be? What are the physical features of your world? What does it look like? Sound like? What is in the environment? What can a player do? What resources are there to hunt for and fight over? Is it a magical world? What is the technology?

Even if you want to set your game in "reality," you have to decide on the tone you want, based on your theme. The *Grand Theft Auto* games are set in a present-day "realistic" world, but one that is stylized by the cynical behavior of its populace and by the darkly satirical outlook of its creators.

MAKE YOUR MAP

Just as you might "card out" the structure of a screenplay, you might want to map out your world. Think of your map as the game board for your story. Where will your hero be traveling to today?

Who Lives There? Who's Paying Rent? Who's The Boss?

Does your game feature one playable character (like *God of War* or *Tomb Raider*), or can players choose from a range of characters or avatars? These characters are all part of the world of the story and it is up to you to know all of those worlds and all of those characters. Who lives in your world? How do folks get around? Or don't they? What are the divisions—geographical, philosophical—between the races/religions/species/sexes? What is the hierarchy of the world? Are there rules? Laws of the land? Each race will have its own history. Its own powers. Write it out. Start building your bible.

Who Am I? Why Am I?

In the chapter on characters, we wrote about developing the main character. A writer is the first player of the game and should not just be asking, "Who am I?" He or she should also be asking, "What am I?" What is the backstory for the protagonist(s)? What is their goal? What do they want? Why? Who are the NPCs, the sidekicks, the rivals, the comic relief? What is their attitude toward the main character?

FILLING YOUR TOOL BOX

Word and images are the tools that screenwriters use to tell their stories. The writer can put an image on the page that conveys exposition and information to the audience. A man might be returning home from work. The shot can switch for an audience reveal that his crazy brother is waiting for him with a rotary sander, cackling maniacally. The audience has learned a piece of information and feels suspense. What will happen next?

The toolbox for the writer of interactive fiction is a lot larger than that of the playwright or the screenwriter. There are many unique tools that we as video game writers have at our disposal. But no matter what tool we use, it is always toward the same end: keeping our players involved in our story. This does not mean you need to spoon-feed the player every piece of information. Give the audience clues. Let them figure out that 2 + 2 = 4. Don't tell them. Let the exposition unfold as the story unfolds. This is breadcrumb storytelling.

Shuffled Nuggets: Backstory as Gameplay

When you drop what seem like random bits of information throughout a level or throughout the game, it becomes a puzzle for the player to piece together enough of the information to understand what has come before. You're telling the backstory in shuffled nuggets. The players assemble the story in their heads, so it becomes storytelling as gameplay, which can be much more satisfying, even though it seems chronologically disjointed. This is not a new thing. We've seen it in prose. We've seen it in movies such as *Pulp Fiction* and *Memento*. We see it a lot in exploration games like *Dear Esther* or *Serena*. In *BioShock*, telling the backstory of Rapture's fall through the (optionally) collectible audio tapes is very effective, and effectively creepy. Like Hitchcockian horror, the images the audience assemble in their heads are more disturbing than what could ever be shown in-game.

Every story is a mystery, or it should be. Not matter what tableau you are using to tell your tale, stories should ask questions. What is going to happen next? Why is this happening? What is really going on? Why did she do that after I asked her not to? As the story unfolds, or the players proceed through the game—they should be gathering "breadcrumbs," following a narrative trail toward information and conclusions.

Boxes

By this, we don't mean smashable crates; we mean the box that the game is physically packaged in. This is a tool that is rapidly disappearing, as we move steadily toward digital downloads. Like good cabinet art on arcade machines (see *Centipede* and *Missile Command* for great examples), a good game box could tell you a lot about the game's world and mood, beyond just the glossy screenshots on the back of the package. Nowadays, the "game box" is becoming a tiny thumbnail of artwork next to the game's title on the long list in the digital download store. Like vinyl album covers, we will mourn the eventual demise of beautiful game boxes.

Loading Screens

A loading screen is what displays while a new level is loading into the computer's memory. These are great opportunities for writers to convey story material to the audience. Loading screens *can* have gameplay tips and hints, but when done effectively they help to keep the player immersed in the game world if they keep the player thinking about the story and the world. Loading screens might have quotes from characters in the game; they might have information about what lies ahead. But what might otherwise be a blank screen becomes an opportunity to keep your players "in the moment."

Interactives

Phones calls, newspapers, journals, photos, letters on the ground that a player picks up and examines are all *interactives*—sometimes *clickables*, or *collectibles*. Clues to the story, or in the case of *BioShock*'s audio tapes, the backstory. Players of the detective game *L.A. Noire* quickly learn that every item an NPC leaves behind is more information about the story.

G.U.I.

Graphical User Interface is the onscreen stuff you see that mediates between you and the game world. It's the information you need—like a mini-map, a health bar, or an ammo counter—that tells you your player state during the gameplay. It tends to take you out of the game world (and game developers have been working for years to minimize persistent GUI, make it more pleasing to the eye, and even hiding it until the player calls it up). However, GUI can become another way to help tell the story. Some GUI might be very relevant and important to the story line at that moment of game time, or it might be backstory filling out the world. Players in *Mass Effect* can call up the player menu and read as much as they want about the rich history of every world they explore and the history of the known universe. One of our favorite GUI motifs is the Pip-Boy 3000 wearable computer in *Fallout 3* and *Fallout: New Vegas*. It's the player menu, sure, but it's themed out and called up as if mounted on your left forearm, which in the game world, it is.

Text Blobs

These are very conventional. When you click on a quest giver in an RPG, you have read the quest requirements, but these are always given in the context of the story of what the quest giver needs, and how it's relevant to the game world. We call these *readables*. The problem is, they're *boring*. There can be space constraints, legibility can be a problem. This is true in *Myst,* where there's a lot of text on the screen, but in bitmaps of handwritten cursive writing on parchment that looks like a copy of the Declaration of Independence that has been left out in the rain. It is very hard to read. In *World of Warcraft* there are tons of books you can read that give you lengthy backstory about various characters and events that shaped the *World of Warcraft*. And there are in-game achievements you can earn for reading all the books. But you shouldn't have to bribe the players to engage with the world backstory—the *lore*—of your game.

Voice Prompts

Go to a station, activate a computer screen, and a message might play. It might be read out loud. It might have to be read. Click on an NPC—they might tell you more of the story. In *Portal,* GlaDOS is an unreliable narrator. She is as untrustworthy as Keyser Söze was in *The Usual Suspects.*

Voiceover is very conventional, and once we get to the scene with voiceover, the player thinks, "Ahh, voiceover! I know what's going on here." The problem is it's *telling,* not *showing.* The voiceover is presented really well, however, in *BioShock* and some other games.

Dialogue

Dialogue is a primal storytelling technique. Whether it's dialogue overheard by or engaged with the PC, dialogue is very straightforward, emotional storytelling. But it can be very costly, because someone has to do the casting and recording and pay all the people involved. Then, if you're selling in foreign territories, you've got an exponential cost, as you've got to translate the script and hire talent to re-record those lines in the appropriate languages. If you're going with simple subtitles in non-English territories, that can be less costly, but it's still not free.

Plus, there's a dilemma with interactive dialogue: it has to be written to anticipate all possible responses from the player. For instance, if you go up to a quest giver in a role-playing game, the minute they start repeating themselves, the "fourth wall" breaks and the experience stops being immersive. Following is a very, very simple quest giver dialogue tree.

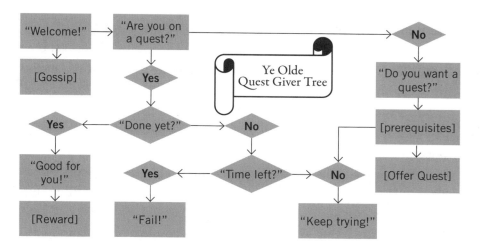

As you can see, if you have any sort of lengthy or repeated interaction with this NPC, you're going to hear dialogue repeated in a way that no feeling human being would repeat dialogue. That is a problem that developers are still learning to design around.

Props and Set-Dressing: Reading the Tea-Cups

Props and set dressing are among the most effective ways you can convey story information. Unlike movies, where you have to hold the camera on visual clues, and you risk breaking up the flow of a scene or sequence, games can allow each player to move and observe at his or her own pace. Players can move around more or less at will, so it's a much more interactive experience. The player gets the joy of discovering the information rather than passively receiving it. In the infrequent lulls during the action of *Left 4 Dead*, you can search the safe houses for handwritten messages from other survivors.

The downside of conveying story information through the environment is that it's easy for players to miss, unless you do something to make such information obvious (like with a floating arrow or a shimmering border), and then you lose the immersion. So, this tool is best kept for lore and not so much for mission-critical information that the player must know in order to advance through the level.

CINEMATICS. OR CUT THE CUT SCENES!

One of the most popular games of 2008 was cooperative zombie shooter *Left 4 Dead*. Is there a story to the game? We say that there is, but the story is not the plot, because plot is very basic: kill zombies to survive. The story is the world, a city in chaos where you're thrown into the action with four teammates. You don't know each other. You have to learn to cooperate to survive. Part of the fun of the story is to try to figure out how the world slid into zombie apocalypse mode. Valve, the developer of *Left 4 Dead*, makes clever use of some of the tools of storytelling that we have discussed.

What it doesn't do, except in the very beginning, is use cut scenes. There is *one* cut scene in the beginning that is kind of the tutorial. That's it. You're then thrown into the action and left to fend for yourself, literally.

The Brass Age of Cinematics

Cinematics are probably the most common tool when you talk to a bunch of game developers who aren't versed in writing at all. They tend to want to shove all the storytelling into the cinematics, because they understand movies and trust the cinematic to be a point when they can just talk at the player and reduce player interaction. We've seen some examples, like in *Metal Gear Solid 4* and *Assassin's Creed*, where during a long dialogue scene with lots of exposition you have minimal control over on-screen action. You can make things in the environment jiggle in *Metal Gear Solid 4*. You can make your player character run around and do fighting moves while he's being lectured to in *Assassin's Creed* while listening to a mission briefing. But, it's not meaningful. It does not change the outcome of the game or the story.

So, cut scenes are traditional non-interactive movies. The good thing about them is that they're very conventional, and the audience understands almost immediately that this is a story moment to which they should pay attention. The downside is they're non-interactive and players have notoriously short attention spans, and they get very twitchy. There's a reason they're playing a game and not watching a movie—they want to be able to interact with what's on screen rather than passively watch it.

Writing Great Cinematics

The conventional wisdom is that players hate cut scenes and want to skip through them. Our challenge to game writers is always to write scenes good enough to hold players' interest so that they won't want to skip through them. Make the characters three-dimensional, make the visuals interesting. There's a real opportunity for good writers who understand both cinema and games to be able to continue to improve the quality of cut scenes.

Brian Kindregan, a lead writer at Blizzard, has said that cinematics help to humanize characters, something you don't get from watching sprites move around the screen. Cinematics take players out of the basic world map and bring them into the heart of the action, allowing players to experience the "maximum amount of impact" of the story's emotions.[56] We agree. For stories to improve, cinematics must improve. We must change these from *skip over* to *must see* and here are some ways to do so.

Make Sure Your Cut Scene Can't Be Cut

The first question to ask is why are you writing a cut scene? If it's just to show off a cool world, you can do that during the gameplay. Your cut scene has to do at least one of the following. If it does all three, even better!

Move the Game Narrative Forward. Cut scenes should push the story forward. Things need to happen. You'd be surprised how many cut scenes are fillers that add to the exposition, but not the story. Good

---

56 http://www.polygon.com/2013/3/31/4158872/cinematics-emotionally-connect-players-to-game-narratives-says

cinematics are the highlight reel, not the news report.

Reveal Character. Cut scenes in the age of facial motion capture allow us to convey—via performance—the emotional state of our characters. What motivates them? What are their "ghosts?" Why are they acting this way?

Provide One Piece of Crucial Audio/Visual Information to the Player. A cut scene might task PCs with what they need to do, or where they need to go. The longer the information conveyed, the duller the scene. For example, if the mission briefing is for the player to go find a baby lost in an orphanage, the best use of the cut scene is to show us and let us hear the baby. The rest of the info—where the orphanage is, which windows are unlocked, which security guards like to leave their post and vape—is best conveyed on the fly in voiceover, text, or some other means.

Who Wants What?

Scenes should be like small battles (or negotiations, or seductions). Someone should win; someone should lose. Always think about who wants what in the scene. Does your character want information? That information is the *exposition* needed to push the narrative forward. Exposition earned is better than exposition given. We think scenes fail when too much exposition is given up too easily. If someone wants something in a scene, then that should be balanced with someone not wanting to give it.

Setup and Reaction

Movies are big events. Things happen. The motley crew in *Guardians of the Galaxy* breaks out of prison. They have a big fight scene—a "set piece." Think of the gameplay in terms of big set-pieces except you, the player, get to be a part of them. For example, imagine any of the *Fast and the Furious* movies. The vehicular action scenes are terrific fun. They are exhilarating. In interactive narrative the player feels and experiences the exhilaration. Here is where the cut scenes come in. Cut-scenes should be *setup* and/or *reaction* scenes. They should set up the gameplay (battle) that is about to happen. Think of them like a scene before a big event in a movie that might have a boxing match, or a wedding. We see the *setup* scenes to learn how the characters are feeling going into battle—what their expectations are like. There, we see the action. Here, you play the action. A setup scene primes and motivates the player.

A *reaction* scene shows the emotional reaction and aftermath of the gameplay that just happened. Did someone die in combat? Have your protagonists react to it in the cut scene. Are they angry? Doubtful about what they are doing? Good! Have them be nervous; afraid; confused. Have them *reacting* to the situation that is unfolding around them. This grounds the character emotionally, as well as the game.

What Is the Whammo?

Here is what usually happens in a good scene: a character wants something, but something happens that spins the story in another direction. A good rule to remember is that when expectations are met, things get boring. There is a great moment early on in *BioShock* where you can finally see the submarine that is your ticket out of Rapture. You've spent several levels and hours of gameplay just to get to this point. As you approach the sub . . . IT BLOWS UP! This is a WHAMMO! The producers of *Die Hard* talked about how every 10 minutes a movie needs a *whammo*; something that spins the story into a new direction. In a game, you need the *whammo* to spin the story on to a new mission, a new quest, or new level.

SOFTWARE FOR GAME WRITING

Please use screenwriting software. You will need to it to write cinematics. There are plenty of free programs—as well as **Word** templates—that allow you to automate the very strict formatting that film and television requires. (And yes, most cinematic scripts are written, and rewritten, like screenplays.) We have used **Final Draft** (finaldraft.com) for years for our script projects, and it's generally accepted as the industry standard. We have also used **Celtx** (www.celtx.com), and it also works well. At the time of this writing, however, these are strictly screenplay packages and do not support a lot of the other formats you'll need when developing a video game.

For video game dialogue, the industry has for years used **Excel**, Microsoft's ubiquitous spreadsheet program, although any good spreadsheet program will do, such as **Google Sheets** or **Numbers for Mac**. A spreadsheet's versatility at both formatting text and performing low-level database functions makes it uniquely suited to writing non-liner, procedurally generated video game dialogue.

There are some relatively new programs that are aimed specifically at the needs of narrative and content designers. **Chatmapper** (www.chatmapper.com) looks very promising, especially for non-linear dialogue. **Articy:draft** (www.nevigo.com/en/articydraft/overview) is billed as game design software and story software all in one.

ACTING AND DIALOGUE—BARKING UP THE WRONG TREE

There's nothing more annoying to us than when a game reviewer complains about "bad voice acting." There's no such thing as bad voice acting. Their beef (though they don't know it) is with *bad dialogue*. And that's not the fault of the voice actor. Blame should be shared by the writer and the production process.

Writing game dialogue is very complex. The traditional game production process works *against* good dialogue.

Remember that in most games, even huge AAA titles, the amount of traditional, linear dialogue scenes are dwarfed by the amount of non-linear, procedurally played dialogue. These are called "barks." They're tough to write, hard to direct, very hard to perform, and are often the focus of fanboy carping about "bad voice acting."

Pay attention to spoken audio the next time you're playing a game. In the middle of a level, although you might encounter an NPC or kill a mini-boss that triggers a cut scene, for the most part the dialogue you hear—whether from your PC or an NPC—is triggered by something that happened in the game. Remember our discussion of "if, then" statements? Let's suppose we're playing a first-person shooter about public accountants—*Audit Squad!*—where your PC is part of a four-person team moving through enemy territory (a rival firm's offices). Some states you might find yourself in include:

- You find ammo
- A squad mate finds ammo
- You find a health pack
- A squad mate finds a health pack
- You spot an enemy
- A squad mate finds an enemy
- You take fire
- A squad mate takes fire
- You are wounded
- A squad mate is wounded
- You die
- A squad mate dies
- An enemy spots you
- An enemy takes fire
- An enemy is wounded
- An enemy dies

So, without trying very hard, we've identified 16 different states you might find yourself in playing this game. Now let's write some barks:

- You: "I found some ammo!"
- Squad Mate 1: "I found some ammo!"
- Squad Mate 2: "I found some ammo!"
- Squad Mate 3: "I found some ammo!"

Even in four different voices, this would get dull very quickly. Let's add some variations just for the PC:

- "There's some ammo!"
- "Look, an ammo clip!"
- "Awesome! Ammo!"
- "Just what I need!"

Does that seem like a lot to you? Think of how many ammo pick-ups the designers will place in the level, and how many times you'll find them every time you replay the level (sometimes by choice, sometimes because you have to start over). Are five different versions of "I found some ammo!" enough? Are ten?

Now remember that you've got your three squadmates finding ammo as well. So we should write ten variations for each of them, right? This is a lot of spoken lines! How the heck are we supposed to keep track of all of them?

Now you're beginning to see why game dialogue expands exponentially. Game dialogue is mostly written (and always tracked) in a spreadsheet or database. Barks often seem repetitive, generic, or both. How do you write ten different ways of saying, "I found some ammo!" in a particular character's voice? (How do you make Squad Mate 1's lines sound like Squad Mate 1 but not Squad Mate 2?)

How do you make each sound distinct? How to you keep each as short and concise as possible, while still being "flavorful?"

This is a problem for the writer. But it's also a problem for the programmer, the gameplay designer, the level designer, the audio engineers, and the voice actors (remember them?).

Actors train in the theater. They learn to read linear scripts. They learn to improvise. They learn to play off one another, both verbally and physically. They are taught (in America, where the Method still reigns) to live in the emotional truth of the moment.

Now, take that same classically trained actor, put him in a booth—alone—with a list of lines to speak on a spreadsheet. If he's lucky, there's a column next to the spoken line explaining the mood he should convey (e.g., "frightened"). If he's really lucky, the writer or creative director is in the recording session next to the engineer, available to answer questions and help to "direct" the session.

But the voice actors are very often not that lucky. Screenwriters have it lucky in a way, they only have to write one tough guy line. Game writers have to write dozens, and they all:

- Have to seem in the "voice" of the character (PC or NPC).
- Have to be brief.

Clint Eastwood's "Do I feel lucky? Well, do ya punk?" or Samuel L. Jackson's Ezekiel 25:17 riff only work in the context of the longer monologues they appear in. The longer a game character's line of dialogue, the longer it pulls a player's focus from the gameplay.

Ideally, dialogue should convey what the character is feeling at that given moment.

Good dialogue, in a game or on film, is the emotional DNA of the characters. It reveals who they are. Smart people like to show off with SAT words. Clever people play jokes off what the other has just said. People with strong group identification like to use the patois of that group. The more carefully you study good dialogue, the better your characters will sound.

Good dialogue is both *concise* and *precise*. It resembles good joke writing. You've got so little time to convey so much information. As Brad Pitt cautions in *Ocean's Eleven,* "Don't use seven words when four will do."

USE THE WORLD FOR WORDS

We often like to set our games in imaginative worlds. Try using imaginative (but still understandable) speech patterns and vocabulary. Special worlds should have special languages. Likewise, historical settings deserve historical speech patterns and language. However, try to see if you can do something more imaginative than pseudo-Elizabethan diction (full of "thees" and "thous") delivered in campy English accents. There's nothing worse than warmed-over Shakespeare. Let Shakespeare be Shakespeare; let you be you.

Building Your World

IN THE OPENING PAGES of a screenplay, television show, novel, and game, there is nothing more important than establishing the world of the story. But how do we build the world? We talked about bringing it to life. How can you do that?

1 COMPLETE YOUR WORLD-BUILDING CHECKLIST

Thinking of these questions will help you write the backstory of the world of Your Game, or its "lore." In your Game Journal, answer the following questions:

1. What is the HISTORY of my world?
2. What is the TECHNOLOGY or MAGIC (If any) of my world?
3. Who are the INHABITANTS of my world?
4. What is the CULTURE of my world?
5. Are there CLASS DISTINCTIONS? DIFFERENT RACES? What is the HIERARCHY?
6. What do the Inhabitants EAT? Do they HUNT?
7. What is their RELIGION?
8. What are the different COUNTRIES? CITIES?
9. What are the LANGUAGES?
10. What is the CURRENT SITUATION in my world? Is it a time of war? Peace? Fear? Calm?

Your world doesn't have to be as big as a *world*. It can exist at any scale you choose. If your game takes place on an abandoned space station, the same questions apply. What is the history of the space station? What technology is on it? Who lived there?

2. Write Your Opening Scene

A well-written introduction can bond the player to the characters and the world of Your Game. *Fallout 3* opens with Ron Perlman rasping "War. War never changes." *BioShock* opens with a plane crash in the middle of the Atlantic Ocean. *The Last of Us* opens with a birthday scene between father and daughter. These are *hooks* designed to grab the player.

We want you to write the hook for Your Game. Conceive a scene that will grab the player and get them excited to play the game so that they can guide the PC on their quest. What can you do in the scene that gets the player thinking, "What happens next?" How do you introduce the gameplay? How does the scene point the players in the right direction so that they know the objective of the first level?

(Again, use screenplay format.)

CHAPTER 10

WE ALL CAN'T BE BATMAN: ON MMO'S AND MULTIPLAYER

WHEN *DC UNIVERSE ONLINE* was announced a while back, we were very excited. We like DC Comics, we like MMOs (that is, Massively Multiplayer Online games). But we both wanted to play as Batman. Our friends said, "no, you can't do that." "Why not? He's on the box! I wanna play as Batman, dammit!" They patiently explained that the way the game was designed, the big DC superheroes were NPCs, and we would have to roll our own superhero—Algebra Dave, or whoever— and be Batman's lame-ass protégé. This wasn't very satisfying. No one wants to be a sidekick. (Ask Robin). Everybody wants to be the hero of the game.

Just as in the *Star Wars* MMOs, where we can't play as Darth Vader, or *World of Warcraft*, where we can't play as Arthas, Thrall, or any of the main characters in that world, we had to accept that MMOs tend to be big shared playgrounds, costume parties, theme parks. Every player is living out his or her own fantasy, including you. This is also true of traditional multiplayer games, whether the competition is head-to-head (*Madden*) or team vs. team (*Counter-Strike*), or a free-for-all (almost any first-person shooter).

(An exception to the "We Can't All Be Batman" rule is, at the time of this writing, the Marvel MMO *Marvel Heroes 2015*, where you and dozens of other players *can actually be* Spider-Man, or Hulk, or Thor. It's narratively incoherent, and the screenshots look like a cosplay show gone horribly wrong, but at least you get to play as your favorite Marvel hero.)

"SPEL" TIME

The Swedes, among others, have more than one word that means "play." *Spel* means, generally, to play a game; to participate in a rule-defined entertainment activity. But they have another word, *lek*, which means to play in a less structured fashion; to frolic, to pretend.

If you've ever seen kindergartners at recess, you'll notice they're running around, pretending, chasing each other, throwing what can be thrown. They typically lack the attention span to engage in rule-defined playground games like kickball, freeze tag, red light/green light, etc., unless an adult is there to act as both announcer and referee. And even then . . .

Think of it also as the difference between playing with the big Christmas toy that Santa brought you versus playing with the box it came in. The box can be a dinosaur cave, a castle, a space ship . . . anything you want it to be.

We've had networked digital playgrounds for a while now: Multi-User Dungeons (MUDs), MMOs, games, chat rooms. And the problem is, with multiple users, you're not just dealing with Mario vs. Aristotle. You (the writer) and the player are coauthoring the player's experience along with a host of others: other players, guild mates, n00bs, griefers, campers, gankers, bots, and gold farmers.

When you have multiple players coexisting in the same environment, competing agenda are inevitable. In a multi-user environment, players are not controlling protagonists; they're playing avatars of themselves. It's the players themselves who are running around the many maps *of Call of Duty: Modern Warfare 2*, wreaking havoc, and not Soap, one of the protagonists of its single-player campaign. Many players will insist that multiplayer games and virtual worlds are more immersive because it's them in the world, not their avatars. But sometimes the experience can amount to kindergartners putting on a show and needing a timeout for unruly and undisciplined play, or in this case, narrative.

The simple truth is that the presence of avatars controlled by actual human beings in a game space is more exciting to many players, and that presence distracts players from the narrative design. Why? Multiplayer environments tend to enhance:

Competition—because it's more challenging to defeat wily human beings than predictable, computer-controlled "bots,"

Social Connection—because it's fun to chat and plot with teammates, as well as to trash-talk opponents, and

Aggression—because, see "competition" above. Bots don't corpse-camp or bully after they kill your avatar. Teenage boys full of acne rage will.

But if the presence of other players trumps the attention that would otherwise be paid to the story you've so deliberately crafted, what's a game writer to do?

WHOSE STORY IS IT, ANYWAY?

The job of the narrative designer in cases such as these is not so much to tell a story as to plan a party. Or create a playground. Or design a theme park attraction. Or, in the case of big games, serve as Julie, the cruise director from *The Love Boat*. You're setting the table and creating a bunch of engaging content that gives players a reason to come in and mingle with each other as they play with the toys you've laid out.

The Walt Disney Company has long called its theme park creators "Imagineers," and with good reason—they're creative geniuses. They will scour every corner and every detail of every space they create at the Disney parks—whether it's a big ride or a passageway between shops—and are always thinking about how they can "theme" that detail. How can this thing reflect the story of the "world" (or "land," as in Frontierland, Tomorrowland, etc.) in that part of the park? At a Disney park, the top of a stanchion is almost never a plain metal ball. In the Haunted Mansion, the stanchions are gargoyle heads. In other rides, the stanchions are "themed" to reflect those attractions. This obsessive attention to detail is what has kept people coming back to the Disney parks for half a century. There is always something new to notice.

As game creators, we can learn a lot from the Imagineers. Video game artists are wonderfully creative, but they can't be expected to imagine everything about the game world. Ditto with all the other creative teams. It's up to the narrative designer to fill in the "imagination gaps" in the story, in the world, in the levels. Otherwise your game isn't a Disneyland—it's a Six Flags.

SANDBOX GAMES

Sandbox games are games where the player is free to roam about the world, interacting with objects and possibly other players. They may or may not follow the rules of conventional game storytelling. There may or may not be numerous quests that can divert or distract the player. These flesh out the world and the game. (Niko dating or having bro time in *Grand Theft Auto IV* does this.) The idea is the more the player interacts with the world, the richer the player's experience. *Ultima VII, Dead Island, Borderlands, Fallout 3*—all these can be considered sandbox games. They still have a main narrative, but the writer needs also to write for all the other quests and missions that a player can choose to experience.

MULTIPLAYER GAMES AND MODES

As we've stated, you're not writing a story, you're throwing a party (or acting as cruise director) with games like *EVE Online* and *World of Warcraft*. The story is the theme of the party. It is the backdrop. And like parties, these games are designed to be social. There are clear story goals—players team up and go on missions, go zone to zone. If done well (*Blizzard!*) players will pay a monthly fee to continue to live in these worlds. As we write this, *WoW* recently celebrated its tenth anniversary.

The main quest of an MMO—the meta-story—is always a variation on "max my level!" Anna Anthropy has described *World of Warcraft* as "a game about performing repetitive tasks until numbers increase." This is very true. The story is *all* side quests. These comprise the lore of the game world. Players often learn as much or more about the game world from other players as they do through direct interaction with the game. The narrative designer's job is to continue to come up with story-based ways to make the repetitive tasks seem not so repetitive.

The writer's other job is to *relax*. If you're ever thrown a party, you know that not everyone is going to love everything: not all your guests will get along with your other guests, not every person is going to sample every delicacy you spent hours in the kitchen slaving over. That's okay. If everyone had a memorable (and positive) experience, they'll think you're a good host—even if they remember very different things about your party.

EMERGENT GAMEPLAY AND EMERGENT NARRATIVE

Emergent gameplay means basically that the player has discovered a means of using the game's mechanics and systems to create gameplay that the developers may not have intended. For example, keeping Dogmeat alive in the original *Fallout* or racing in two-car Saleen/MINI Cooper "Cat and Mouse" teams in *Project Gotham Racing 2*.

We can attest from personal experience that the minute you discover — either by accident or Internet—that you can turn a swing set into a trebuchet in *Grand Theft Auto IV,* your interest in Niko's rise through the ranks of Liberty City's criminal underworld grinds to a halt. You immediately jack whatever vehicle is at hand and head straight for the nearest swing set. The narrative then loses its focus on Niko and becomes about you showing anyone who will pay attention how you can make a car launch into the troposphere.

Emergent narrative, then, is motivating the fun of emergent gameplay with stories that you create yourself. You, the player, are writing you own story. There's a superb example of "emergent narrative" in the classic 1980 comedy *Caddyshack*. Bill Murray's character, Carl the groundskeeper, is tasked with changing some flowerbeds. We see him with a grass whip, but, because the movie takes place in and around a country club, Carl decides to turn his work into a game by pretending the tool is a 2 iron and the flowers are golf balls. He narrates each swing, providing the play-by-play as he decapitates the flowers: "The crowd is standing on its feet here at Augusta . . ." (This narrative seems even more emergent when you learn that it was improvised on the set by Murray—his lines weren't in the original script!)

The player's story may lack the direction and emotional resonance that you, the writer, intended players to have. But players are in control of their own experiences. Truly invested players—those who have bought into the world you've created—will write biographies of their avatars, create fan art and fan fiction rooted in your world. It is, like all imitation, the sincerest form of flattery you as a creator can receive.

Emotional Resonance

Emotional resonance is a very Aristotelian concept. It fits on our journey of emotion. We the players are engaging in "reflective empathy." The protagonist is onscreen. I am doing the things that I think are best for him. My avatar feels the emotional results of my actions, but I do not.

When Will Smith killed his dog in *I am Legend* (SPOILER: he had to!), we cried, but we didn't feel the bullet go into our own heads.

Emotional Presence

The word *immersion* begins with the letter I. *I'm* in the game. *I*, the player, am doing the things that I want to do. I own the emotional results of my actions. Here's an example:

AERITH DIES. BOB CRIES.

(This story contains a big fat SPOILER about *Final Fantasy VII*. Deal with it.)

You are emotionally present in the game when your feelings as a player reflect the feelings of the protagonist(s) in the game world. This is very hard to do, and it certainly won't happen with *every* player, but it's something we should continually strive for as game creators. One of the earliest and best examples of such a moment that we can remember is when Bob was playing the classic Japanese RPG *Final Fantasy VII*.

In the story of the game, the player character Cloud Strife meets and adventures with a group of misfits that includes Aerith, the flower girl in the long pink dress. She and Cloud fight together, she's kidnapped by the bad guys, Cloud and the team rescue her, they go on a date. Their relationship is the main love story in the game, and after the first date, Bob kept waiting for another lull in the action to see if they had a second date, or beyond . . .

In the gameplay, Aerith is the healer of your party. *FFVII*'s combat system pits three of your characters – typically Cloud, Aerith, and a third hero – against a group of bad guys. No matter how low your team's health got in the early parts of the game, Aerith could be counted on to cast her Healing Wind spell and bring your party back from the brink. At this point in the game, as a player, you could concentrate on learning how to use your weapons and magic to do damage to your opponent with near impunity. You could count on Aerith to keep you healthy.

Which is awesome, until you have an encounter—in a non-interactive cinematic—with the game's main villain, Sephiroth. He stabs Aerith through the heart with his huge sword. She dies. You watch. And, because this happens in a non-interactive cinematic, there's *not a damn thing you can do about it.*

At this point, Bob cried. He'd spent hours upon hours with Aerith. He watched Cloud flirt with her; he watched her flirt with Cloud. He, like Cloud, depended upon her to do the healing when they fought bad guys. And now she was irreversibly dead.

In the game's story, Cloud is stricken with grief. In real life, Bob was stricken with grief. He shed a few tears for Aerith. He turned off the game for a few days. He mourned her. He mourned the fact that he'd have to learn how to heal his party himself, rather than relying on her. Bob felt *emotionally present* in the game, even though he was away from it. The PlayStation was turned off.

Moments like this are what we as game creators should constantly be striving for.

———

MULTIPLAYER OFTEN COMES FIRST

In many games that feature robust multiplay modes, the multiplayer game itself is designed first. Then, toward the end of that process, the designers create the "story" or "campaign" mode, i.e., the single-player game. The oversimplification is that with many FPS and RTS games, the single-player game is a long, elaborate, story-driven tutorial for the multiplayer game. And certainly with many games this feels true.

Bob was a longtime fan of RTS games such as *World of WarCraft, StarCraft, Command & Conquer* and *Age of Empires.* At Mattel Interactive, he was excited to work on the RTS games *Earth 2150* and *Warlords: Battlecry*—albeit late in the process.

Several months later, he was tapped to be lead tester on *Battle Realms*, a cutting-edge 3D RTS from developer Liquid Entertainment set in a fantasy world based loosely on Japanese mythology. He was shocked, however, to learn that the game they were testing lacked story mode. The bulk of the development time was spent implementing, debugging, and balancing the core "build & battle" RTS gameplay. The campaign ("story mode") was added much later in the development cycle, barely 90 days before the release of the game.

On the MMO project they worked on together, Bob brought Keith in to bring story to the project and to enrich the world of the game. This was, however, after months of development of the core game systems, which combined action sports gameplay in an MMO-style virtual world. After months more work by Keith and the rest of the team, however, that game was ultimately scrapped. But, oddly, the story survived and the parent company considered pitching it as a television show.

Games need to be fun. And it's fun to go to a party. But the party usually winds down, someone gets upset, someone gets into a fight and leaves early—welcome to MMOs. Sandbox games are not MMOs. With sandbox games—story rules. As it always should.

DRAGON EXERCISES 10

Feeling Your World

1 MAP THE EMOTIONS OF YOUR GAME

As we've said, there's room for improvement when it comes to invoking a wide range of emotions in games. In Your Game, what emotions will the PC feel at various stages? What emotions will the player feel? Write an "emotion map" of Your Game that discusses ways in which the emotional journey of the PC can correspond to the journey of action that the player will progress through.

2 WRITE A DLC CONCEPT

Downloadable content (DLC) and other post-release content is growing more and more popular as players and creators realize the value of extending the play experience—and the story—of the game beyond its "end." Just because Niko Bellic's story was over in *Grand Theft Auto IV* didn't mean that the world of Liberty City couldn't support the rich stories of its DLC releases *The Lost and Damned* and *The Ballad of Gay Tony*.

MMOs, in particular, live and die by the popularity of "expansions" that not only expand the horizons of their virtual world, but also introduce new characters and story lines for players to enjoy.

Let's pretend the publisher asks you to produce a DLC episode for any game you like. Choose an existing game and create a short (three or four paragraph) pitch for a DLC expansion of the world in the game. You can create new characters. You can make use of new locations. The trick is: Can you capture the spirit of the original game?

CHAPTER 11

ALWAYS BE CREATING

THE RISE OF THE INDIES

On the other end of the business spectrum, one of most exciting but least discussed trends in the last decade has been the destruction of the traditional barriers to entry for game development. Prior to the launch of the App Store and the spread of popular "game processors" like GameSalad Creator, games were made by a very small, very specialized, and very homogeneous class of people—career game developers. It's no surprise that these folks tended to create games that appealed to themselves (science fiction, medieval fantasy, combat action). As games became more and more commercial (and more and more expensive to make), games by and for Sheldon Cooper types were always an easy bet for publishers over something risky that broke the mold and was innovative either in its gameplay or its story. You can probably count on one hand the exceptions (*The Sims*, *Guitar Hero*) that prove this rule.

But after the turn of the twenty-first century, something very cool happened. Small teams started to develop "garage games" and distribute them directly to players through sites such as newgrounds.com and kongregate.com. Although most of these games were perhaps a step back in cutting-edge technology—many were authored in Flash and playable in web browsers—they helped to create a culture of independent games that quickly exploded as digital distribution and self-publishing matured thanks to the advent of the Steam PC download service and the mobile app stores.

Now some of the most expressive, innovative, and popular games (ever heard of *Minecraft*?) are coming from independent developers

WHO ARE THE GAME PLAYERS?

"Player satisfaction consultants" International Hobo have created a very useful model called BrainHex, which surveys and sorts player types into one or more of seven categories: *Seeker, Survivor, Daredevil, Mastermind, Conqueror, Socializer,* and *Achiever.* You can take their survey and discover your own player type at survey.ihobo.com/BrainHex.

—

or individual creators. (Yes, Microsoft bought *Minecraft*, but that was after—and because—it became a global phenomenon.)

As we write this, the broader US games community is still dealing with the fallout of the ugly #gamergate controversy. What ostensibly started as an online movement "concerned with ethics in game journalism and with protecting the gamer 'identity'"[57] became a controversy regarding sexism in video game culture that included vile on-line attacks and real life threats against game developers Zoe Quinn, Brianna Wu, and many of their supporters. In the late summer and fall of 2014, the threatening behavior of a tiny minority of hardcore game enthusiasts—the so-called "real gamers"—revealed them to have the emotional maturity of the He-Man Woman Haters Club from the old Our Gang shorts produced by Hal Roach.

Not all video game players self-identify as "gamers," just as not all motorcycle owners self-identify as bikers. As we said in the very beginning of *Slay the Dragon*, more people enjoy video games than ever before. Different players play different games for different reasons. We need to stop thinking of "gamers" as one massive self-similar, culturally congruent hive-mind.

A full two years before #gamergate, however, Anna Anthropy published what we believe to be an antithesis and antidote to the entire affair. Where the #gamergaters were narrow and exclusive, and chauvinistic, and insular, and focused on the traditional games-as-a-consumer-product

---

57 http://gawker.com/what-is-gamergate-and-why-an-explainer-for-non-geeks-1642909080

model, Ms. Anthropy's book was the reverse: broad, inclusive, and promoting games as self-expression and therapy. In her book, *Rise of the Videogame Zinesters: How Freaks, Normals, Amateurs, Artists, Dreamers, Dropouts, Queers, Housewives, and People Like You Are Taking Back an Art Form*, she wrote that:

> There's nothing unnatural about a digital game by an individual creator (or a pair of creators). It is, in fact, much harder to keep the idea behind a game coherent when the designer is managing a team of many people who are each working on one aspect of the game separately. That's part of the reason why contemporary big-budget games have so much clutter and so few strong ideas.[58]

If we had a nickel for every time we heard someone in Hollywood bemoan that same problem about big-budget movies, we could . . . finance our very own AAA game!

In the meantime, and in the spirit of self-expression, exploration, and fun, we want you to make your own interactive experience. It's not as difficult as it seems. No programming or art skills are necessary! Just have a story to tell and play.

TOOLS YOU CAN USE

There's no reason you can't use this book as your springboard to start working on your very own game today. We get frustrated with screenwriting students who complain that they can't work unless they buy expensive screenplay formatting software. You can write a screenplay if you have a pen and paper. It's the ideas that matter; the format can come later. We get similarly frustrated with students who complain that they can't start making games unless they have extremely expensive graphics software, 3D animation tools, and programming environments. This, too, is bunk.

You want experience in interactive writing? *Write something interactive!*

---

58 Anthropy, loc. 1613 of 2813

Here's how:

START ON PAPER

Turn off the computer. Get a note pad. Get a pencil. (Get some index cards!) Make some notes. Doodle. Diagram. Daydream.

The more thinking you do before you fire up the tools, the more productive your tool time will be. Card it out. Work out what you want to express and *how the player will experience that*. Remember, the players are the coauthors of their experience, but they can only act within rules that you create. What are those rules?

This may seem counterintuitive. "But games are a digital medium!" you protest. We know. We also know dozens of veteran game designers who prefer paper prototyping because it's easier, cheaper, and faster. We've seen time and again how novice creators will go launch straight into a level editor or other digital tool, and . . . nothing. They're overwhelmed by the interface. They're overwhelmed by the learning curve. They have no idea what to create. They're subject to the tyranny of endless possibilities. They freeze. They choke. (This has happened to us, too. Bob had an opportunity to create a multiplayer map for *Battle Realms*. Rather than do the creative thinking for what his map would be like beforehand, Bob fired up the level editor and . . . well, let's just say that there's no Bob-authored multiplayer map in *Battle Realms*.)

Once you have your concept worked out, then you may turn on your computer and start to work with your tools. What tools? Here are some of our favorites.

EASY MODE

If you haven't tried writing an interactive short story, you should. There's no better way to understand the power and complexity of interactivity and shared authorship than interactive fiction. Write an original short story, or *take a short story you've already written* and reimagine it as an IF story. It's a powerful, frightening process. Do it!

Inklewriter

Inklewriter (www.inklestudios.com/inklewriter) is a free, very easy-to-use, web-based tool that allows you to write a branching story. You can also publish your story on the Inkle Studios site and share a direct link to your story with friends, family, fans, and followers. There are some example stories to read for inspiration as well. (Bob's own IF short story, "Why I Got Divorced," is there at writer.inklestudios.com/stories/vvmb.)

Twine

Twine (twinery.org) is a very popular free open-source tool for both IF and simple text adventure games. It's slightly more complicated than Inklewriter, but you can very easily write a simple branching story to get started. Then you can add images and other features to make your story more game-like as you get comfortable with Twine.

Scratch

Available for free at scratch.mit.edu, Scratch is a graphical "game processor" developed at the Massachusetts Institute of Technology for children to learn the fundamentals of logic and scripting. Because it was designed for kids, it's very easy to start to use to create your first actual game. Scratch is a great gateway tool between writing IF and text adventures to graphical gameplay.

MEDIUM MODE

Ready for a little bit more of a challenge? The following will require some patience, research, tutorial reading (or watching), and trial and error. But the reward is well worth the effort when you see your ideas come to life onscreen and enjoyed by other players.

Games about Creation

Minecraft has changed everything. There's an entire generation of kids and teens for whom creating, scripting, and cooperating in 3D space is as natural as riding a bicycle: once learned, never forgotten. *Minecraft* is well worth your time. It's available on almost every platform—PC, console, mobile—so download it and get crafting.

Explore some of the thousands of special servers and mods out there, or ask any children in your life to give you a tour. We were blown away recently when a friend's bored 10-year-old daughter showed us how to make a working roller coaster, from scratch, on an iPhone.

Don't forget about the *Little Big Planet* series, which is available on PlayStation devices, as well as *Project Spark* and the Toy Box mode in *Disney Infinity*. All of these games are designed to teach you to create your very own playable game content and—in some cases—easily share it with other players. Unlike level editors (below), however, they're designed for kids, have intuitive interfaces, and offer help prompts if you get stuck.

Level Editors

Level editors are sometimes included as a bonus with a retail game; sometimes they're a separate free download. To make a level editor, the development team will typically simplify or polish up the same content creation tool they used to build levels in the game. But they don't spend a lot of time de-bugging these tools, and they seldom have a lot of documentation. You will have to be patient and find tutorials and creator communities to help you get started or solve problems.

We also recommend that you start with an *old* game, rather than something on the bleeding edge. Especially if you're not familiar with 3D tools, working with a 2D level editor will be far less frustrating. Try making a map in *StarCraft* before you graduate to *StarCraft II*.

Portal 2's "Test Chamber Designer" (level editor) is very polished, simple, fun, and a great way to get started, as is the track editor in the gloriously over-the-top motocross racing game *Trials Fusion*.

If you're very ambitious or have some experience with 3D tools, BioWare has a very robust level-, quest-, and cinematic-authoring package that works with the PC version of *Dragon Age: Origins*. The Dragon Age Toolset is a free download,[59] but it only works if you have *DA:O* installed on your computer.

---

59 http://social.bioware.com/page/da-toolset#downloads

One of the best things about any game with a level editor is that you can import and play levels created by other players to get a good sense of how creative you can be.

Game Processors

GameMaker: Studio and GameSalad Creator are two of our favorite "game processors" that bring all the tools to allow you to build a game into one software package. You don't need to be a programmer to create interactivity in a game processor, although the more programming or scripting you know, the more you can enhance your project. We've used both of them in the classroom and been very proud of what our students were able to do. They have robust tutorials, support, and user communities. Both are designed to allow the novice or professional to create a game and publish it on multiple platforms, including iOS, Android, Mac, Windows, and HTML5.

GameMaker: Studio is available as a free download at yoyogames .com/studio/download. The free version of GameSalad Creator is available at gamesalad.com/download.

Although we have not vetted it, we hear good things about Stencyl (www.stencyl.com). It's also free to try.

HARD MODE: GAME ENGINES

Once you are part of a development team—or have a reliable source of programming, artwork, and audio—then you can think about graduating to a commercial game engine. These are professional game development environments and are not for n00bs or the faint of heart. Unity has made great strides as a market leader in recent years, thanks to its relative ease of use and a vast asset story that allows you to buy and use characters, props, terrain, and other assets à la carte to use in your project. You can download the free trial at unity3d.com.

Epic Games' epically powerful Unreal Engine has powered dozens of AAA games in recent years, and with each new release it supports more eye-scalding visuals and gets (again, relatively) easier to use. You can learn more at unrealengine.com.

DRAGON EXERCISES 11

Using New Tools

1 WRITE AN INTERACTIVE SHORT STORY

Using Inklewriter or Twine, write an interactive short story. This can be a story set in the world of Your Game, or in a completely different setting. You could also adapt a traditional, linear short story you've already written into an interactive short story. (Were you torn between writing one ending or another? Now you can include them both!)

To get a good feel for the medium of interactive fiction, your story:

1. Should have at least eight decision points.
2. Can have decisions that branch (e.g., the decisions may lead to further decisions, such that the reader might not hit every decision point in one read-through).
3. Can have multiple endings.

2 BUILD A LEVEL

Using the level editor in a commercial game, like *Portal 2*, *Disney Infinity*, or any of the others we discussed in this chapter, create your own game level.

Plan on paper! Just as you wouldn't begin writing a screenplay without an outline, don't start hacking at the level editor without a plan as to what you want players to do in the level, and what obstacles you can put in their way.

Does the level editor have features that would enable you to include story content? What story could you tell through the design gameplay of your custom level?

3 EXPLORE A "GAME PROCESSOR"

Download, install, and follow the first tutorials in either *Game Maker: Studio, GameSalad Creator,* or *Stencyl*. If you get through the first tutorial, move on to the second. And so on. Congratulations! Now go forth and make games.

CHAPTER 12

WHAT HAPPENS NEXT?

THERE IS NO WAY to predict the future. Well, maybe *Star Trek* could. They had communicators (smart phones), tricorders (tablets), and voice-activated computers. Even *Star Trek: The Next Generation* had the holodeck (a virtual reality game system) and "wearables." But not even James T. Kirk could have ever predicted that an arcade curiosity like *Pong* would evolve into a billion-dollar business.

Here are some common predictions about the future of video games made over the last few years.

- Stereoscopic Gaming (playing in 3D, like a 3D movie)
- Virtual Reality (see above, but you're wearing the screen like googles)
- Secondary Screens for Gaming (like the Wii U)
- Augmented Reality (AR)
- Cloud-Rendered Gaming (like the OnLive game service)

Some of these predictions are over five years old. In this technological age, that is a very long time. So which ones have come true? Cloud gaming is still dealing with throttled bandwidth. We all would not mind a Netflix for games. Second screens? The Wii U didn't set the world on fire. Virtual reality is, as we write this in early 2015, still very buzzy. And with game legends like John Carmack (*Doom, Quake*) touting a near-religious experience when he dons his Occulus Rift glasses[60] —that landscape seems fertile.

Interesting that in the predictions we found there is no mention of the continued rise and influence of indie games, or Apple becoming a big player in the space, or of whispers that Amazon or Google might begin to compete with original game content. That is because we have no way to know what the future of gaming is going to be. A famous quote attributed to many goes like this: The only way to predict the future is to invent it. So with that in mind we give you the future of gaming. Our prediction is this:

The future of video games is story.

THE FUTURE IS STORY

We've discussed the differences between Mario and Aristotle. Facing them off. But for the game industry to grow creatively and to attract the respect and recognition it deserves, Mario needs Aristotle. Do we envision a day when the Oscar goes to the Best Game? Or Best Interactive Story? Why not? People never thought animated movies would get their own Oscar—but they do. Once tech and story team up, there are endless levels to explore.

"*Grand Theft Auto* Is Today's *Great Expectations*" is the title of a Nick Gillespie article in *Time* magazine[61] where he makes a compelling argument: sales, popularity, and "uninformed attacks on video games as morally suspect perfectly parallel the rise to cultural dominance of once-derided forms of creative expression such as movies and the novel."

We feel the future has already started. *Star Wars* brought in the age of the Hollywood blockbuster and put the whole transmedia thing into hyper-speed. But the best *Star Wars* story since *The Empire Strikes Back* was not in the movies. The best story might have been the game *Star*

---

60 http://www.bleedingcool.com/2014/12/30/john-carmack-says-experiencing-oculus-rift-like-religion-contact/

61 http://ideas.time.com/2013/09/20/grand-theft-auto-todays-great-expectations/

Wars: Knights of the Old Republic, the ending of which makes the player character choose to embrace either the light side or the dark side of The Force. The story of *The Force Unleashed* was better than that of *Attack of the Clones*.

Halo, Final Fantasy VII, Mass Effect, Metal Gear Solid 3, Snake Eater . . . all feature stories of emotion and action with rich characters and deep lore of the world that only 60 hours of gameplay can fill.

To see more of the future, play the indies: *OctoDad, I Am Bread, Transistor, Kentucky Route Zero, Thomas Was Alone, This War of Mine.* These games are using the mechanics and doing things only games can do: Immerse the player and allow choice.

Immersion and choice and story are the future.

THE WORLD IS FULL OF GAMERS

Story-driven games and immersive entertainment will continue to grow and occupy a greater share of our culture. As William Shakespeare never said: "All the world's a game, And all the men and women merely players." Players have many choices in games: genres, platforms, single- or multi-player. Audiences have many choices for watching TV and movies—on their mobile devices, game consoles, televisions, or in a cinema. Audiences have many choices as to how to talk about anything: social media, chat, e-mail, texting. Even phone conversations. It's a society that is more active in what they do and how they share things. Call it the "Immersive Epoch."

Children who grew up with video cameras in their faces gave rise to YouTube and the Silicon Alley and Silicon Beach digital entertainment companies. They wear FitBits and have brought gamification into their lives, chalking up likes on Instagram as one might rack up points in a game. Video game culture has spread to social activities. Clubs and bars where people meet to play games are growing in popularity. You can walk into an art gallery in New York City and be part of a ten-person game like *Killer Queen*[62]. Or you might decide to be part of an immersive

---

62 http://www.nytimes.com/2014/10/12/nyregion/killer-queen-a-10-person-console-game.html?_r=1

theater experience where the game is very much a video game narrative. Where are we and how do we get out? It's called *Escape the Room* and as the *New York Times* called it, "video game meets real life." [63]

Games will grow in popularity and more and more writers will and should make it their first point of entry. A place where they can have their voices heard by a rising generation that wants to do more than listen. They want to play.

GET INTO THE GAME!

We still call it film school. How much film is used in film school? Not much. Students learn photography with digital cameras. So should we start calling it digital school? No. The name has stuck. Video games might very well follow the same path. We call them video games because that is how they started. *Pong* was a game. Nothing more. No story whatsoever. But games have evolved into such a variety of immersive, interactive entertainment experiences that defining a game by one set of rules is very limiting.

We believe there is room for everyone in this great new art form. There is room for both traditional developers and indies. There is room for games that follow a clear narrative, games that follow no narrative, and games that take us on new emotional journeys, such as *Depression Quest* and *Try Not to Fart*. All voices should be heard and no one should be silenced. Change is good. Change brings innovation. You can be the change. Your voice will help make the art form richer and more diverse.

So how can you get started?

Play Games

Nothing irks us more than people who want to write for the movies, but don't go to the movies. Or people who want to write for television, but don't watch TV. If you want to work in games—*play games!* That is always going to be the best education you can get. Play board games, mobile games, console games, browser games. Read about games. Your

---

63 http://www.nytimes.com/2014/06/04/arts/video-games/in-escape-rooms-video-games-meet-real-life.html

go-to morning read should be Gamasutra.com. Read books about game design, development, and history (not just this one). Attend game conferences and conventions. Chances are there is one in or near your town. Meet other game players and creators. Do anything you can to be around this field.

Find a Game Jam

Game jams are marathon game development sessions in which ad hoc teams conceive, plan, create, and showcase games. They can last 24 hours or up to a weekend; they're grueling but fun, and a great way to network and get hands-on experience at the same time.

Game jams typically happen around schools or through game developer groups. Find one in your area and volunteer. Even if you feel like you have no technical skills, you can still help to brainstorm, playtest, and do the hundred other non-technical things required to make a game on such a tight schedule. A great resource and community hub can be found at www.indiegamejams.com.

Go to School

Stay in school. Or go to school that focuses on game development. The Entertainment Software Association recently announced there were over four-hundred colleges and universities offering courses on video games and the average salary for someone working in video games was $95,000. (Although, in our experience, this is a little high.) *The Princeton Review* even ranks these programs each year.[64] What we see is a movement away from traditional computer programming toward a combination of entertainment and tech. Learn story and learn programming. Or art. Or sound design. Or music composing. Or marketing . . .

Go to Work

If you're too cool for school, or already have a degree—get to work. Video game companies have entry-level jobs. Bob got his start this way.

---

64 http://www.princetonreview.com/top-undergraduate-schools-for-video-game-design.aspx

Testers, for example, are people whose job is to test games, find bugs, and write up the steps so that programmers can fix them. You can start at the bottom and work your way up. Gamasutra.com is a great resource for all things video games and always has an up-to-date job board. Other entry-level jobs include customer service representative and community manager.

Make Games

Any self-styled creator should always be creating. You need to create the fire because it burns in you to be a creator, and because it's a great way to get noticed and work your way up in any creative field. Television writers cannot produce twenty-four episodes of a television show on their own. So how can they get their work seen? Write a play. Character and dialogue are the keys to good television writing. James Gunn, the director and cowriter of *Guardians of the Galaxy* made low-budget indie movies long before he brought Groot to life. Check out his movie *The Specials*.

An aspiring game writer/designer/producer/creator has to be making games. Games are made to be played and enjoyed and now there are so many ways to do that.

OUR FINAL CHALLENGE TO YOU

We've made many assertions in these pages. You may quibble with some of them. We hope you agree with most of them. They are all based on our mutual (yours and ours) desire to push the interactive medium forward toward its inevitable maturity. And we don't just mean that video games are more than fifty years old, which *Spacewar!* certainly is.

What drives that maturing of games is not the evolution of technology, but rather their ability to reflect the full spectrum of human emotions. They can enable us, through gameplay, to experience and to identify with and to understand those who *are not us*. This is what the best art does, no matter what medium. And all art conveys a narrative. An artist has a story to share. As we mentioned, there are many critics who do not believe video games will have a place at the adult table of art. These critics' ancestors had the same thing to say about another art form—the movies.

214 **SLAY THE DRAGON**

To put this in context, let's look back at when film entered its fifth decade. Pioneering media scholar Marshall McLuhan's most famous quote was that "the medium is the message." If true, then certain media have an innate ability to deliver certain emotions in an easier and more direct manner than do other media. Let's call these "native emotions."

The native emotions of cinema can be seen simply by looking at the earliest film genres: comedy, suspense, romance, horror, and westerns (which could feature a wide variety of emotions). And so the film medium chugged on for decades—on both sides of the Atlantic—as pop culture for the mass audience, comfortable entertainment in uncertain times.

But World War II changed everything. Smaller, more mobile cameras, along with cheaper and more portable sound recording technology greatly reduced the barriers to entry for filmmakers around the globe. These filmmakers emerged in the fifth decade of the motion picture medium, having largely grown up watching films themselves. Sweden's Ingmar Bergman, Japan's Akira Kurosawa, Italy's Roberto Rossellini and Vittorio De Sica, France's Francois Truffaut and Jean-Luc Godard, and many others operating outside the traditional studio model were able to make more personal films that expressed a wider range of emotions than had ever been explored. Audiences now could experience despair, torment, shame, lust, and alienation. Moviegoers went to these films to be challenged rather than comforted. American filmmaker Paul Schrader once said that Bergman "probably did more than anyone to make cinema a medium of personal and introspective value." It's not surprising that the movies made by Bergman and others of his generation became known as "art films."

We are confident that the next wave of game creators will help to create more personal games that will challenge players' emotions, not just their skills. We see it already starting. You stand at a moment in history when it has never been easier to create a game. Use this moment to create games that allow players to experience and understand emotions that are not comfortable, that are complex, that reflect the often maddening puzzle that is the human condition.

Make games that reflect *your* experience and worldview. Add your unique voice to the medium. Regardless of your gender, ethnicity, sexuality, culture, or class—or perhaps *because* of it—your voice should be heard. Your thoughts should be shared. Your emotions experienced by other players who *are not you.*

As much as we as film buffs respect the late Roger Ebert, he was wrong in one crucial instance. Video games *are* art, and their capability for artistic expression grows every year.

Our challenge to you, and our deepest wish, is that you will take some of what we've discussed in these pages and *use* it. Go forth and *Always Be Creating.* Make your mark on this medium. Make games of "personal and introspective value" that will last for generations to come.

Now go slay that dragon!

Bob & Keith out.

Bringing it Together

1 WRITE YOUR GAME CONCEPT DOCUMENT (GCD)

As we discussed earlier, there's no such thing as a "spec script" for a game. You can, however, put together a Game Concept Document that, like a movie treatment or a series bible, serves as a discussion document and a creative reference. They're also a good portfolio piece, in that they are themselves mini portfolios. Yours should contain:

- *Title*. This should seem obvious. A good title is your first foot in the door. A bad or perfunctory title says to your reader that the concept is bad or perfunctory.

- *Cover Page with Artwork*. Never mind that you're not an artist. Borrow something that evokes the mood or setting you're trying to convey. (Don't make it a famous image, though, because then all your reader will be thinking about is the original work, not your work.)

- *Executive Summary*. This is your GameFly Pitch. Tell me who I am, where I am, what I get to do, and why.

- *Genre and Core Game Mechanics*. What are the main play mechanics?

- *Platform*. Be as broad as possible. Is it for consoles? Mobile? PCs? You're concerned here with how the user will play the game, rather than how it will be sold (e.g., boxed retail vs. via a download store.)

- *Concept (gameplay/story) Summary.* This is a longer description of both the story and the gameplay. One page maximum. Be sure to discuss how the story reflects the gameplay, and vice versa.

- *Gameplay Description.* Briefly discuss how this game plays differently from and better than similar recent hits in its genre.

- *World Description.* Players will be spending a lot of their time in your game's world. Why is it exciting? Different? Dramatic? Worthy of their exploration?

- *Protagonist Brief Bio.* Also those of key NPCs and Bosses.

- *Description of Your Game's Beginning.* How will you start so that the player is hooked from the very beginning? How do you plan to keep them playing?

- *Game Structure/Level Outline.* Expand upon the concept summary by giving a level-by-level description of the story beats and gameplay progression in each level (or mission, or quest, etc.). This will give your reader a sense that you have a definite shape of the player's experience in mind, as well as a sense of the scope of the entire project.

- *Gameplay Highlights.* What do I get to see or do in the trailer? What's awesome about your game that will have one player telling another player to try it (on the school bus, or around the break room)?

- *Sample Cinematic Script.* (optional)

- *Sample Barks in your character's voice.* (optional)

Keep this short (no more than about twenty pages). It's a sample. It's also not a Game Design Document (GDD)—those can be hundreds of pages long. Those document the decisions the department heads have made about the game they're making. GDDs end the conversation. GCDs *start* the conversation.

Again, your GCD is not something you'd be able to get an agent with or shop around to game publishers. But it's a great portfolio piece. Plus, you never know . . .

Glossary of Select Terms
from Video Game Production and Culture

"Try and keep up with the acronyms."
—Agent Simmons (John Turturro), *Transformers*

AI. While this ostensibly stands for artificial intelligence, it is often used interchangeably with NPC (see below). AI can also refer to the scripted behavior of any computer-controlled character or monster.

Asset. See Game Asset.

Bark. Non-linear, procedurally played, stand-alone lines of dialogue.

Beta Testing. Testing done by players outside of the development team—sometimes the general public—on a pre-release version of a game (the "beta" version). Beta testing is typically used to fine-tune the game as well as to find (and fix) the remaining set of bugs.

Boss. An extra-hard adversary or enemy. Typically placed at the end of a game level (a "level boss") or in the game's final encounter (the "game boss").

Bot. From robot. A computer-controlled character that fills the role of player in a multiplayer game.

Casual. This term is used to describe games that are relatively less demanding of a player's time, effort, and dedication to play or enjoy. "Pick up and play" is a cliché often used in reference to casual games.

CGI. Computer-generated imagery.

Class. This typically refers to the game mechanic that an RPG character is best suited for. Playing a healer class means you're best at keeping your teammates' health replenished during combat. Playing a fighter class means you're best at dealing damage to enemies.

Console. A proprietary computer system designed and sold primarily for playing video games. The Xbox One, PlayStation 4, and Wii U are all consoles.

Core. See Hardcore.

Cosplay. Costume play—creating and wearing a costume based on your favorite video game or other character from popular culture. Cosplayers like to congregate at conventions.

Cut Scenes. Noninteractive (or minimally interactive) dialogue or action scenes that are used to advance the game story.

Engine. See Game Engine.

Flavor Text. Any non-gameplay-critical information that helps to contextualize, or add "the flavor of the game," to player instructions. On a card from *Magic: the Gathering*, it's the evocative story content in italics at the bottom. On a *World of Warcraft* quest, the flavor text tends to be in the "Description" section. Although flavor text is not the most immersive game content, it's certainly the easiest to create.

FPS. "First Person Shooter." A shooting game in which the player is on the ground and the camera is at eye level with the player's character. Examples include *Doom, Quake, Unreal, Halo,* and *Call of Duty*.

Game Asset. (Or simply Asset.) Any part of the game that the player can see, hear, read, or otherwise experience in a game is an asset. Lines of dialogue, animations, textures, objects, GUI (see below), loading-screen artwork . . . these are all assets. The game writer's work product is generally text assets, some of which may be recorded as dialogue, which then become audio assets.

Game Engine. (Or simply Engine.) The core set of software instructions (code) that makes a game run.

GCD. "Game Concept Document." This is a short "game treatment" that serves as a discussion document to articulate a vision for a game. Contrast with GDD (see below).

GDD. "Game Design Document." This is the exhaustive "bible" that describes each and every aspect of what the entire development team will build. The best of these are "living" documents or wikis that can be easily searched and updated as the game evolves. Sometimes accompanied by a Technical Design Document (TDD) that describes to the programmers the technical aspects of the game, such as the rendering system or physics engine.

GUI. "Graphical User Interface." The menu systems and onscreen data—like mini-maps, countdown timers, and health bars—that display important information to the player but which are not part of the game world.

Hardcore (or "Core"). This term is used to describe games that require significant time, effort, and dedication to play or to complete, as well as to describe those players who play them. See antonym at "Casual."

Indie Game. A game conceived and developed outside the traditional game publishing model. These (typically smaller-scale) games are made without publisher financing or publisher control.

IF. "Interactive Fiction." Branching-path prose stories (or even novels) that require the reader to make choices in order to continue reading.

IP. "Intellectual property," which is protected either by a patent (for technical IP-like inventions) or copyright (for creative works). An "original IP" is a story or brand that has never been seen before in any medium.

IRL. "In Real Life." That space between game sessions in which players must (presumably), eat, sleep, use the toilet, bathe . . .

Live Team. The development team (or a subset of them) responsible for maintaining an online game once it has been released, or "gone live."

Loot. Prizes or money you collect from an opponent you have just defeated.

Lore. The backstory of the game world.

Meatspace. See IRL.

Mission. See Quest.

MMO. Massively Multiplayer Online game. We prefer this to MMORPG (Massively Multiplayer Online Role-Playing Game), as not all MMOs are RPGs.

Noob. (Also "n00b" or "newbie.") A new, unskilled player, hence an easy target.

NPC. "Non-Player Character." This term can be reasonably applied to any computer-controlled character, but typically refers to characters with whom the player can interact via dialogue or other means (like vendors or quest givers) beyond simply killing or being killed.

PC. "Player Character." The character you control in a game. Contrast with NPC.

Quest. An in-game task, to be accomplished for a reward. Typically assigned to the player by an NPC.

RPG. "Role-Playing Game." In an RPG, players create their own character based on a set of physical attributes, skills, personality traits, and other metrics, then go on long adventures comprised of shorter quests. The table-top game *Dungeons & Dragons* was the first wildly popular RPG.

RTS. "Real-Time Strategy." A war game (like *StarCraft* or *Age of Empires*) in which players gather resources, build armies, and attack other players. Gameplay occurs simultaneously for all players, as opposed to by turns, as in traditional table-top war games or turn-based computer games like *Civilization*. Because everyone plays at once in an RTS, speed and reaction time are very important.

Shooter. A game in which the primary mechanic is aiming and shooting, like *Galaga*. See FPS.

Sim. Short for "simulation." Many games are computer simulations of real-world systems, where the gameplay comes from operating or managing the system. The "gameplay" in the *Microsoft Flight Simulator* series is flying a non-combat airplane in real time from one airport to another. *SimCity* allows you to control the infrastructure of a city and watch the impact of your actions on the city's growth, or lack thereof. *Roller Coaster Tycoon* is a theme park management simulation. Realistic sports and racing games are sometimes called sims.

SNES. Nintendo's classic Super Nintendo Entertainment System console, released in North America in 1991.

Tutorial. That content which teaches a player how to play the game. The best of these are transparent and happen on the fly as the player explores the game world (see *Grand Theft Auto IV*). The worst are stand-alone "boot camp" levels that force the player to learn every mechanic early in the game, even though some may not be available until much later.

WOOt! A cheer of victory of approval. Thought to be derived from "we owned the other team."

WoW. Short for *World of Warcraft*.

About the Authors

ROBERT DENTON BRYANT has worked in Hollywood in marketing and production, and in video games as both a publisher and a developer. He has been the executive producer of dozens of games on platforms ranging from CD-ROMs to the iPad, including the best-selling *World Championship Poker* and *Pinball Hall of Fame* console franchises. He is the coauthor (with Charles P. Schultz) of *Game Testing All-in-One*. He has guest lectured on game writing at universities in the United States and Europe, and continues to teach in the Writers' Program at UCLA Extension as well as at Woodbury University in Burbank, California. You can follow him on Twitter @thumbcandy.

KEITH GIGLIO has worked as a screenwriter and producer on such feature and television movies as *Joshua, Noah, Return to Halloweentown*, Walt Disney's *Tarzan, Pizza My Heart, A Cinderella Story* and *Another Cinderella Story*. He has written for Paramount Pictures, The Walt Disney Company, Universal Studios, Warner Bros. Pictures, Spyglass Entertainment, Walden Media, Tokyopop and Platinum Studios. His book *Writing the Comedy Blockbuster* was published in 2012. He also loves video games and has worked as a narrative designer for the in-house game development studio of a major toy company. Keith currently teaches screenwriting and video game writing at the Newhouse School at Syracuse University. You can follow him on Twitter @keithgiglio.

Photos courtesy of Terri DePaolo (top) and Juliet Giglio (bottom)

SAVE THE CAT!®
THE LAST BOOK ON SCREENWRITING YOU'LL EVER NEED!

BLAKE SNYDER

BLAKE SNYDER

BEST SELLER

He's made millions of dollars selling screenplays to Hollywood and now screenwriter Blake Snyder tells all. "Save the Cat!®" is just one of Snyder's many ironclad rules for making your ideas more marketable and your script more satisfying — and saleable, including:
- The four elements of every winning logline.
- The seven immutable laws of screenplay physics.
- The 10 genres and why they're important to your movie.
- Why your Hero must serve your idea.
- Mastering the Beats.
- Mastering the Board to create the Perfect Beast.
- How to get back on track with ironclad and proven rules for script repair.

This ultimate insider's guide reveals the secrets that none dare admit, told by a show biz veteran who's proven that you can sell your script if you can save the cat.

"Imagine what would happen in a town where more writers approached screenwriting the way Blake suggests? My weekend read would dramatically improve, both in sellable/producible content and in discovering new writers who understand the craft of storytelling and can be hired on assignment for ideas we already have in house."
> – From the Foreword by Sheila Hanahan Taylor, Vice President, Development at Zide/Perry Entertainment, whose films include *American Pie, Cats and Dogs, Final Destination*

"One of the most comprehensive and insightful how-to's out there. Save the Cat!® is a must-read for both the novice and the professional screenwriter."
> – Todd Black, Producer, *The Pursuit of Happyness, The Weather Man, S.W.A.T, Alex and Emma, Antwone Fisher*

"Want to know how to be a successful writer in Hollywood? The answers are here. Blake Snyder has written an insider's book that's informative — and funny, too."
> – David Hoberman, Producer, *The Shaggy Dog* (2005), *Raising Helen, Walking Tall, Bringing Down the House, Monk* (TV)

BLAKE SNYDER, besides selling million-dollar scripts to both Disney and Spielberg, was one of Hollywood's most successful spec screenwriters. Blake's vision continues on *www.blakesnyder.com*.

$19.95 · 216 PAGES · ORDER NUMBER 34RLS · ISBN: 9781932907001

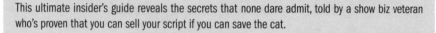

24 HOURS | **1.800.833.5738** | **WWW.MWP.COM**

WRITING THE COMEDY BLOCKBUSTER
THE INAPPROPRIATE GOAL

KEITH GIGILIO

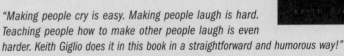

Dying is easy, comedy is hard. So keep your comedy blockbuster alive and well and buy this book. Comedy has always
been the backbone of the film business. In an age of sequels
and brand-name movies based on established properties, the
original comedy screenplay still delivers high profits. *Writing
the Comedy Blockbuster* guides the writer as they learn what
goes into writing the next comedy classic.

*"Making people cry is easy. Making people laugh is hard.
Teaching people how to make other people laugh is even
harder. Keith Giglio does it in this book in a straightforward and humorous way!"*
> — Alan R. Cohen & Alan Freedland, Writers/Producers of
> *Due Date, King of the Hill, American Dad*

*"It'll light a fire under your ass — and not in a teen comedy kind of way. Inspirational,
practical, and a great read unto itself. Keith's book will help you write not only a great
comedy screenplay but also any genre of screenplay."*
> — Michael Davis, Writer/Director of *Shoot 'Em Up,
> Eight Days a Week*

*"This book is not only about Blockbuster Comedy... it reads like one! Sharp, funny, and
focused on the practical and commercial, Keith Giglio has crafted the essential handbook
for writing modern film comedy — for anyone ambitious and twisted enough to try!"*
> — Tom Brady, Writer/Director of *The Animal, The Hot Chick,
> Bucky Larson: Born To Be A Star*

KEITH GIGLIO grew up in New York City in a family that felt like the cast of a Woody
Allen movie starring Robert Deniro. His love of film comedy began at an early age. After
graduating New York University's Tisch School of the Arts, Graduate School of Film and
Television, Keith moved to Los Angeles because he didn't want to miss the riots. He began
writing with his wife, Juliet, and they sold their first four scripts, thus forcing them to
work together. He is a member of the Writers Guild of America and has had 6½ movies
produced and many more optioned. In addition to writing and producing, Keith teaches
screenwriting at Syracuse University.

$22.95 · 229 PAGES · ORDER #176RLS · ISBN 9781615930852

THE WRITER'S JOURNEY
3RD EDITION

MYTHIC STRUCTURE FOR WRITERS

CHRISTOPHER VOGLER

BEST SELLER
OVER 170,000 COPIES SOLD!

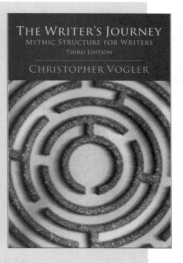

See why this book has become an international best seller and a true classic. *The Writer's Journey* explores the powerful relationship between mythology and storytelling in a clear, concise style that's made it required reading for movie executives, screenwriters, playwrights, scholars, and fans of pop culture all over the world.

Both fiction and nonfiction writers will discover a set of useful myth-inspired storytelling paradigms (i.e., "The Hero's Journey") and step-by-step guidelines to plot and character development. Based on the work of Joseph Campbell, *The Writer's Journey* is a must for all writers interested in further developing their craft.

The updated and revised third edition provides new insights and observations from Vogler's ongoing work on mythology's influence on stories, movies, and man himself.

"This book is like having the smartest person in the story meeting come home with you and whisper what to do in your ear as you write a screenplay. Insight for insight, step for step, Chris Vogler takes us through the process of connecting theme to story and making a script come alive."
> – Lynda Obst, Producer, *Sleepless in Seattle, How to Lose a Guy in 10 Days;*
> Author, *Hello, He Lied*

"This is a book about the stories we write, and perhaps more importantly, the stories we live. It is the most influential work I have yet encountered on the art, nature, and the very purpose of storytelling."
> – Bruce Joel Rubin, Screenwriter, *Stuart Little 2, Deep Impact,*
> *Ghost, Jacob's Ladder*

CHRISTOPHER VOGLER is a veteran story consultant for major Hollywood film companies and a respected teacher of filmmakers and writers around the globe. He has influenced the stories of movies from *The Lion King* to *Fight Club* to *The Thin Red Line* and most recently wrote the first installment of *Ravenskull*, a Japanese-style manga or graphic novel. He is the executive producer of the feature film *P.S. Your Cat is Dead* and writer of the animated feature *Jester Till*.

$26.95 · 300 PAGES · ORDER NUMBER 76RLS · ISBN: 193290736x

SAVE THE CAT! GOES TO THE MOVIES

THE SCREENWRITER'S GUIDE TO EVERY STORY EVER TOLD

BLAKE SNYDER

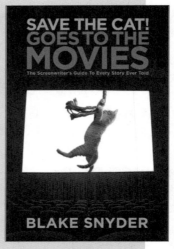

In the long-awaited sequel to his surprise bestseller, *Save the Cat!*, author and screenwriter Blake Snyder returns to form in a fast-paced follow-up that proves why his is the most talked-about approach to screenwriting in years. In the perfect companion piece to his first book, Snyder delivers even more insider's information gleaned from a 20-year track record as "one of Hollywood's most successful spec screenwriters," giving you the clues to write *your* movie.

Designed for screenwriters, novelists, and movie fans, this book gives readers the key breakdowns of the 50 most instructional movies from the past 30 years. From *M*A*S*H* to *Crash*, from *Alien* to *Saw*, from *10* to *Eternal Sunshine of the Spotless Mind*, Snyder reveals how screenwriters who came before you tackled the same challenges you are facing with the film you want to write — or the one you are currently working on.

Writing a "rom-com"? Check out the "Buddy Love" chapter for a "beat for beat" dissection of *When Harry Met Sally...* plus references to 10 other great romantic comedies that will make your story sing.

Want to execute a great mystery? Go to the "Whydunit" section and learn about the "dark turn" that's essential to the heroes of *All the President's Men*, *Blade Runner*, *Fargo* and hip noir *Brick* — and see why ALL good stories, whether a Hollywood blockbuster or a Sundance award winner, follow the same rules of structure outlined in Snyder's breakthrough method.

If you want to sell your script and create a movie that pleases most audiences most of the time, the odds increase if you reference Snyder's checklists and see what makes 50 films tick. After all, both executives and audiences respond to the same elements good writers seek to master. They want to know the type of story they signed on for, and whether it's structured in a way that satisfies everyone. It's what they're looking for. And now, it's what you can deliver.

BLAKE SNYDER, besides selling million-dollar scripts to both Disney and Spielberg, is still "one of Hollywood's most successful spec screenwriters," having made another spec sale in 2006. An in-demand scriptcoach and seminar and workshop leader, Snyder provides information for writers through his website, *www.blakesnyder.com*.

$22.95 · 270 PAGES · ORDER NUMBER 75RLS · ISBN: 1932907351

THE MYTH OF MWP

In a dark time, a light bringer came along, leading the curious and the frustrated to clarity and empowerment. It took the well-guarded secrets out of the hands of the few and made them available to all. It spread a spirit of openness and creative freedom, and built a storehouse of knowledge dedicated to the betterment of the arts.

The essence of the Michael Wiese Productions (MWP) is empowering people who have the burning desire to express themselves creatively. We help them realize their dreams by putting the tools in their hands. We demystify the sometimes secretive worlds of screenwriting, directing, acting, producing, film financing, and other media crafts.

By doing so, we hope to bring forth a realization of 'conscious media' which we define as being positively charged, emphasizing hope and affirming positive values like trust, cooperation, self-empowerment, freedom, and love. Grounded in the deep roots of myth, it aims to be healing both for those who make the art and those who encounter it. It hopes to be transformative for people, opening doors to new possibilities and pulling back veils to reveal hidden worlds.

MWP has built a storehouse of knowledge unequaled in the world, for no other publisher has so many titles on the media arts. Please visit www.mwp.com where you will find many free resources and a 25% discount on our books. Sign up and become part of the wider creative community!

Onward and upward,

Michael Wiese
Publisher/Filmmaker